Risking Faith

John Guest Accelerated Growth Series

Other books in this series

Risking Faith

Personal Answers for Weary Skeptics

John Guest

Foreword by J. I. Packer

BakerBooks

A Division of Baker Book House Co
Grand Rapids, Michigan 49516

© 1993 by John Guest

The first edition of this book appeared in 1983 under the title In Search of Certainty.

ISBN: 0-8010-3854-5

Published by Baker Books
a division of Baker Book House Company
PO Box 6287, Grand Rapids, Michigan 49516-6287

Printed in the United States of America

Unless otherwise indicated, all Scripture in this volume is from the Revised Standard Version of the Bible, copyright 1946, 1952, 1971, and 1973 by the Division of Christian Education of the National Council of the Churches of Christ in the United States of America.

Chapters 8 and 9 of the present work appear in a slightly different version in Beating Mediocrity.

To my wife,
Kathleen,
and our children:
Carrie Anne
Chelsea
Jonathan
Sarah
Susanna

Contents

Foreword

Christians in evangelism sometimes express doubts as to whether honest doubters exist. This is because they meet many professed doubters who are not honest, whose doubt turns out to be a smoke screen, masking unwillingness to face Christ's call to the costly changes that discipleship involves. One can, of course, keep doubting forever if one sets one's mind to it, but willful doubt—doubt for doubt's sake, in order to avoid the commitment that certainty would require—is no more respectable than any other form of willful evasion. John Guest knows, however, that not all doubters are like that, and has written this book for the doubter who is willing to lose his doubts when grounds for certainty appear. It is a good book, clear, persuasive, friendly and trustful, stating the Christian case in the way in which honest doubters need to hear it.

I spoke of "the Christian case," as if there is only one. Does it make sense to say that, when Christendom is split into a four-figure tally of denominations and weird and wonderful novelties are constantly broached in God's name on radio and TV? Are Christians anything like agreed, at basic level, on what real Christianity is, and how you put it into words? Yes, many are, and the world needs to realize that the differences between Christians are on secondary matters and assume agreement as what is primary—namely, that we are creatures made for God who have lost touch with Him, and that Jesus Christ, the man of Galilee, is God come to save us from our lost condition. John Guest's concern is with these primary matters. His book stands in the tradition of the patristic apologies and C. S. Lewis's Mere Christianity, giving reasons for basic-level belief and inviting faith in Christ the living Lord.

If there are reasons for faith, then unbelief itself must be open to doubt. If the case for Christianity is cogent, then the case for noncommitment must have holes in it. While it is true (as John Guest, and I, with all Christian teachers everywhere, acknowledge) that you cannot argue people into faith, nor turn faith into reason without remainder, it is also true that agnosticism about Christian certainties, whether dogmatic and generalized ("no one can ever know") or merely personal and provisional ("I at this moment don't know") is a resting place that is somewhat arbitrary, as well as being somewhat comfortable.

John Guest asks agnostics to think along with him about life, and about Christ. It is not that he has anything new to say to them, though he says old things with a freshness that may make them sound new; it is rather that he sees continuing wisdom and force in the old arguments that Christians have used since the faith began, just as he sees continuing power and glory in "the old, old story of Jesus and His love." So he marks out the old paths once more. That is precisely the strength of his book.

English by extraction, like myself, and formerly rector of a large Episcopal parish near Pittsburgh and sustainer of a widespread evangelistic ministry in addition, John Guest knows human nature, and is able to address honest doubters with forthright gentleness and great charm. The time you spend letting him share his faith with you will not be wasted. He wrote this book to help you to a transforming trust in Christ the Saviour. I commend it to you; I think he did his work well. If we hear that the book is doing its job, both he and I will rejoice; and I expect to hear that soon. God be with you who read it.

J. I. Packer

I Stand by the Door

by Samuel Moor Shoemaker

I stand by the door.
I neither go too far in, nor stay too far out,
The door is the most important door in the world—
It is the door through which men walk when they find God.
There's no use my going way inside, and staying there,
When so many are still outside and they, as much as I,
Crave to know where the door is.
And all that so many ever find
Is only the wall where a door ought to be.
They creep along the wall like blind men,
With outstretched, groping hands.
Feeling for a door, knowing there must be a door,
Yet they never find it . . .
So I stand by the door.

The most tremendous thing in the world
Is for men to find that door—the door to God.
The most important thing any man can do
Is to take hold of one of those blind, groping hands,
And put it on the latch—the latch that only clicks
And opens to the man's own touch.
Men die outside the door, as starving beggars die
On cold nights in cruel cities in the dead of winter—
Die for want of what is within their grasp.
They live, on the other side of it—live because they have
   not found it.
Nothing else matters compared to helping them find it,
And open it, and walk in, and find Him . . .
So I stand by the door.

Go in, great saints, go all the way in—
Go way down into the cavernous cellars,
And way up into the spacious attics—
It is a vast, roomy house, this house where God is.
Go into the deepest of hidden casements,
Of withdrawal, of silence, of sainthood.
Some must inhabit those inner rooms,
And know the depths and heights of God,
And call outside to the rest of us how wonderful it is.
Sometimes I take a deeper look in,
Sometimes venture in a little farther;
But my place seems closer to the opening . . .
So I stand by the door.

There is another reason why I stand there.
Some people get part way in and become afraid
Lest God and the zeal of His house devour them;
For God is so very great, and asks all of us.
And these people feel a cosmic claustrophobia,
And want to get out. "Let me out!" they cry.
And the people way inside only terrify them more.
Somebody must be by the door to tell them that they are
    spoiled
For the old life, they have seen too much:
Once taste God, and nothing but God will do any more.
Somebody must be watching for the frightened
Who seek to sneak out just where they came in,
To tell them how much better it is inside.

The people too far in do not see how near these are
to leaving—preoccupied with the wonder of it all.
Somebody must watch for those who have entered the door,
But would like to run away. So for them, too,
I stand by the door.
I admire the people who go way in.
But I wish they would not forget how it was
Before they got in. Then they would be able to help
The people who have not yet even found the door,
Or the people who want to run away again from God.

You can go in too deeply, and stay in too long,
And forget the people outside the door.
As for me, I shall take my old accustomed place,
Near enough to God to hear Him, and know He is there,
But not so far from men as not to hear them,
And remember they are there, too.
Where? Outside the door—
Thousands of them, millions of them.
But—more important for me—
One of them, two of them, ten of them,
Whose hands I am intended to put on the latch.
So I shall stand by the door and wait
For those who seek it.
"I had rather be a door-keeper . . ."
So I stand by the door.

Acknowledgments

I want to thank the Vestry and members of St. Stephen's Church, Sewickley, Pennsylvania, for the gift of a sabbatical leave which gave me the time to write. The Bodleian Library in Oxford, England, most graciously granted me the use of its establishment for three months in the autumn of 1982, which was an inspiration and privilege. I am particularly grateful to Helen Jean Townshend Elliott, who did all the preparation of the manuscript and constantly encouraged me to get the final draft to the publisher.

Introduction

This book comes out of nearly twenty years of wrestling with agnosticism. Nevertheless it is not written for academia, since then it would be read only by the learned; in any case, I am not the person to write such a book. Rather it is directed toward assisting the many ordinary people who are struggling with what to believe for themselves so that they can direct their daily lives with a measure of assurance.

I write for the businessman who wants sincerely to believe his Christian faith so that he can practice and articulate it with confidence; for the mother who is clinging to her faith and trying to promote Christian standards in the face of opposition from her children who question and challenge everything she says; for the high school or college student who is being "blown away" by sophisticated, quasi-intellectual arguments on the one hand and by the immoral pressure of "everybody's doing it" on the other. I write for average Christians who, while still going to church and believing what they are supposed to believe, have lost the confidence and joy that comes from a sure faith.

There is another very special group of people for whom I write. They are the "communicators" of values at a popular level to our society. Many would be amazed at the confusion, for instance, experienced by the clergy of all denominations who want to speak a sure word of encouragement to their people, but before they open their mouths, and even while they prepare to speak, hear in their minds a cacophony of antagonized response rising from the pews.

15

This is extremely intimidating. There are trade union leaders, scout leaders, YMCA workers, church youth group sponsors, counselors, teachers, public relations offices, newscasters, columnists, politicians, and business leaders who want to influence our society for "good" but who have never managed to sift the clamoring profusion of rival ideas presented to their minds by one special interest group after another.

Advertising also works on all of us; just watch TV, notice billboards, listen to the radio, enjoy popular music, or think about current legislation in the news, and your mind is reverberating with all the variant claims on your intelligence, emotions, and will. If you are in the communicating business in any way at all, I write for you. We need thoughtful leadership that knows why it believes and can help others out of the quagmire that seems to suck them deeper into chaos with every well-intentioned step.

Finally, by way of introduction, I offer this writing that you may become a more convinced Christian. Jesus Christ said, "I am the way, and the truth, and the life; no one comes to the Father, but by me" (John 14:6). Not only does he claim to be the only way to the Father in heaven but he makes it plain that to build our lives on any foundation other than his teaching leads to ruinous conclusions.

"Every one then who hears these words of mine and does them will be like a wise man who built his house upon the rock; and the rain fell, and the floods came, and the winds blew and beat upon that house, but it did not fall, because it had been founded on the rock. And every one who hears these words of mine and does not do them will be like a foolish man who built his house upon the sand; and the rain fell, and the floods came, and the winds blew and beat against that house, and it fell; and great was the fall of it" (Matt. 7:24–27).

There are a number of psychological reasons why, even as you read this last statement by Jesus, you may want to resist it, or feel embarrassed by it. We shall discuss those reasons because it is my conviction that they represent the major reason for the "well-meaning agnosticism" which invades our reasoning.

We don't want our leadership to be as footprints in the sand. I believe it was W. R. Inge who said, "He who marries the spirit of the age will be a widower tomorrow." Not only do we not want to be "ideological widowers," neither do we want our leadership to produce a generation of spiritual orphans. "For no other foundation can any one lay than that which is laid, which is Jesus Christ" (1 Cor. 3:11).

1

Epidemic of Uncertainty

Today we have an epidemic of uncertainty. It is not caused by the threat of a nuclear holocaust nor the shifting sand of international alignments, nor yet by the fickleness of inflation or monetary value systems. Today's epidemic of uncertainty comes from a way of thinking called agnosticism.

You find everywhere people who describe themselves as agnostic—"not to know." These "agnostics" gladly confess that they are uncertain about God. They assert that they have no sure knowledge of God and, therefore, "don't know" what to believe about God. They are not even sure if there is a God. They don't know. They are agnostic.

Now, of course, when you are talking about such a foundational issue as the existence and knowledge of God, and claim ignorance, automatically a legion of other uncertainties becomes apparent. All of them have to do with the spiritual and moral values by which we direct our personal lives as well as our corporate activity. We are no longer simply pondering whether or not God exists. We are now wondering how to affect our society for good, or what to tell our preadolescent children is right or wrong.

Indeed, too many parents have been driven to abdicate any moral influence in the lives of their teenagers because they don't know what to say. Even an extremely respectable group such as Planned Parenthood makes contraceptives available to unmarried students and advocates abortion as an acceptable means of terminating an unwanted pregnancy. Even they do not want to tackle the moral problem of promiscuity. After all, isn't it my body? Can't consenting adults do what they like as long as they don't hurt someone else? The natural response, since there is no sure answer to these questions, is to nullify the difficult consequences of sexual promiscuity. Some will not tackle the real issue of promiscuity because of basically an agnostic attitude to morals. They determinedly fight for what they believe is the moral right of women to the choice of abortion. No wonder there is an epidemic of uncertainty.

Another mark of adult capitulation to the pressures of our culture in the lives of youngsters is the supervised party with alcohol made available for thirteen- through fifteen-year-olds. It sounds so reasonable to say, "Better to let them drink at home under supervision than out in a park where there isn't control." What's a parent to do?

On what basis will we influence lawmakers struggling with the issues of sexuality, pornography, abortion, drug abuse, prison reform, environment, parents' and teachers' rights, unemployment, and international politics? I don't want to give the impression that there are simple answers to these questions. But if we don't know what to believe in the first place, we have nowhere to begin for moral decision making and we become thoroughly confused.

In our confusion we are left with three possible kinds of response: (1) popular opinion, (2) pragmatism, and (3) evasion.

Popular Opinion

When you have no sure conviction, one way to make decisions is to go along with the prevailing wind—blown this way and that by every gust of current thought. With no anchored position you drift with the tide of opinion. How many people are there whose present attitude, you suspect, is that of the last person they spoke to? No doubt the last opinion you heard came by way of the news media. A mighty strong wind blows with their opinion of things. There is little doubt that the general populace is manipulated by the media rather than informed by it.

For instance, on September 6, 1982, while in England I heard on the respectable BBC radio the president of the Liverpool Bible College being interviewed. He had joined a pedophiliac organization—which promotes sexual practice between adults and children—with the intention of finding out from their literature what they were advocating so that he could have firsthand information to pass on to the appropriate government agency to take action.

The thrust of the interview, however, was an implicit attack on the president of the Bible college because he had covertly joined the organization. It was implied to be morally wrong for him, a man who professed faith in God, to "act as a spy."

He made it quite clear that the pedophiliacs did not ask him any questions when he joined the organization, so he didn't have to lie or practice deception.

But still, the interviewer persisted, "Do the ends justify the means?" Of course he denied such a notion. But at the end of the news interview you were not so much horrified that there existed an organization aimed at promoting pedophilia, as you were suspicious that the president had done something wrong in finding them out. By similar innuendoes, opinion drifts from one viewpoint to another, but mostly circles in becalmed confusion.

Too many minds are like water spilled on an oily surface—disconnected attitudes that never seem to come together. No integration, just irregular shapes of thought that bear no relationship to any unity. Easily pushed around but never to form anything around which to develop an identity, family, or community.

Pragmatism

Another way to deal with the confusion that derives from agnosticism is to be practical. That is, case by case, make decisions on the basis of what you think "will work." Again, take the most widely disputed moral issue in the U.S.A.—abortion. From a practical point of view it solves many problems. The mother-to-be, whether married or not, is able to be rid of an awkward and unwanted interruption in her life. When it is an unmarried teenager, parents are also relieved. Those who advocate a halt to the population explosion, and for different reasons there are many of them, are content to let abortion continue because it serves their end very nicely. Those concerned for the poor, and especially the black minority, don't want to see more "unwanted" children raised in poverty to a possible life of crime. In the long term you will reduce the welfare rolls, need fewer prison spaces, and have less of an urban ghetto problem, is the hope.

All these reasons seem so wise and practical, and we haven't even touched the issues of the feminist movement or the enormous medical business that abortion has become. It is so attractive, in the confusion over principles, to opt for a pragmatic solution. It becomes so easy to substitute what is personally and publicly convenient for what is essentially a moral issue of right or wrong.

Evasion

Evasion is the way of least resistance. It allows avoidance of the painful problems already set before us, and many more besides. You can hear the reasons people give for staying neutral: "Who am I to tell someone else what to do?" or, "Religion is a personal thing!" "You don't want to be puritanical, do you?" "Do your own thing as long as you don't hurt someone else."

I have heard religious leaders in a position of some prominence seriously advocate a kind of moral laissez-faire in the optimistic notion that civilization as a whole will right itself. They suggest that in the ebb and flow of human affairs, like the proverbial cat, society will land on its feet! It is not hard to see how each of these agnostic responses in its own way creates more confusion and further spreads the epidemic of uncertainty.

But in addition there appears to be a willing ignorance of the destructive effects of such evasion. Arnold Toynbee's analysis of civilization is a salutary reminder. He says there have been twenty-one civilizations prior to ours. All twenty-one had five distinct stages: (1) birth, (2) rapid growth and expansion, (3) conservation of gains, (4) moral decay, and (5) disintegration (Arnold Toynbee, Stages of Civilization).

For Reflection and Discussion

1. What do you think has (or have) the most immediate influence on ideas and morals?
   a. parents
   b. teachers and schooling
   c. opinions and attitudes of friends and associates
   d. television, newspapers, magazines, advertising
   e. government legislation and propaganda put out by the special interest groups and their lobbying
   f. the church
2. What one thing could each of us do to be opinion makers ourselves, rather than a reflection of others' opinions?

2

Quest for Truth

There has been an age-old quest for what is true, or, to be more mystical, for "the Truth." The real question today is as follows, "Is there a truth that is true for everybody, that is, not just my personal truth, my own point of view, but a truth that measures every point of view and by which you can know if your understanding of things is correct?"

There was a day when the person on the street would have answered, "Yes, there must be an overarching truth that really is the truth for everyone and not just my personal view of things." But that is not so any longer.

There is a tremendously wide variety of thinking today that supports the notion that truth is relative, and your perception of truth is only valid for you. And since most of us have a broad range of information derived from our formal education, as well as casual reading of books and articles, as well as listening to radio and television discussions and talk shows, imbibing philosophies which underlie our entertainment, we are susceptible to this relative way of thinking. Some common phrases used to express this are, "Do your own thing" or, "I'm into my own thing" or, "If it feels good, do it" or, "Don't lay your trip on me."

These are the more contemporary versions of "It doesn't matter what you believe as long as you are sincere." Sunday by Sunday in churches we say the Apostles' Creed. But in reality most people who say it would not mind if you added, "It doesn't matter what you believe as long as you are sincere."

Church people, like many others, have given up on the notion that there really is an "objective truth" which will always be true no matter what one believes, and instead put the emphasis on "sincerity." Validity of faith then moves from the "truth" believed to the "quality of belief" exercised, irrespective of what is believed. That is, in technical terms, from objectivity to subjectivity; from the object believed to the subject who does the believing.

Having simply stated the problem, we must understand the complex network of feeder streams which end up making a broad river. Or to change the analogy, the patchwork quilt of pieces which makes up a broad covering for the bed of the agnostic mind-set.

Philosophic Basis for Agnosticism

The philosophic support for agnosticism comes from people who have set forth the proposition that all truth is relative to the individual. Those who have believed this most strongly have not believed in God at all. If there is no God who has designed everything and written the score from the top down, then all we can do is try to discern things from the bottom up. The French authors Albert Camus and Jean Paul Sartre have been two of the major proponents of this view of things.

Sartre's play No Exit has as its major theme rejection of a divine being who looks down on his creation and weighs them in the balance against the day they shall have to answer to him. Sartre proposes, rather, a world which is "all there is." This is our only existence. There is no way out into some other existence. It is the focus on "this existence" being all that there is which gave birth to the title Existentialist.

In his book The Plague Albert Camus creates a similar situation. A walled city in North Africa is hit with the bubonic plague. To contain the plague, all the gates are locked so no one can leave. There happened to be a newspaperman visiting that town who desperately wanted to escape the city and return home to his wife. But with all the gates closed and guarded he was trapped inside. The story which unfolds becomes a parable of the "existentialist" view of this world. There is the futility of the medical people trying to cure those with the plague and all the volunteers trying to make the dying comfortable. There are those who sip their wine outside the local cafe and watch the frenzied activity of the various do-gooders. They are reminiscent of today's disengaged observer who simply makes critical and shrewd comments but can never be drawn into the drama. There is the priest in the church praying for divine intervention which never comes. And in the midst of all this the newspaperman scurrying from one authority to another trying to find a way out. But he never succeeds. He cannot beg or buy his way out of the city. Always he is let down and always his hopes are dashed. The only reality is the city and the plague of death which carries all before it.

Camus and Sartre are powerful proponents of a world without ultimate purpose or hope. Their starting point is "no God." Since there is no God, there is no designer. With no designer there is no objective design. Because there is no objective design, there is no objective right or wrong since there is no one on the outside—that is, a transcendent God— to make it so. We are left then to make the most of our existence (existentialism) and to understand it as best we can from the human point of view—secular humanism.

Evolution

Just by way of observation, several other sciences, of which the general populace has a smattering of knowledge, seem to support this view of the world. Evolution of species for one seems to support this view. Evolution of species is set forth as a satisfactory explanation of how life came into being and developed to what now is. Take note that in 1981 there was the Scopes trial in reverse, when the creationists tried to get another theory taught alongside evolution, and their attempt was in effect rejected. It made considerable newsprint because at the heart of it all every one of us perceived that there was a religious struggle to discern what was really the truth. But as it stands, U.S. children in state schools can only be taught one scientific theory of what we call creation, and that view supports the existentialist philosophy.

For it follows if we are part of a big cosmic accident that evolved, given time enough through millions of other accidents, which we call mutations, then we are in reality nothing other than accidents or freaks of nature. If we merely are the products of time and chance then there is no such thing, "objectively speaking," as a "moral imperative"—the phrase of Immanuel Kant to describe the sense of "oughtness" which all of us apparently experience. You cannot say to an "accident" that it ought not to behave badly or that it ought to behave better. In any case, who determines what is bad or better?

So the scientific theory of evolution is patched into the existential understanding of life and produces the slogan "Do your own thing."

The View from Psychology, Psychiatry, and Sociology

There is a commonly held view that what you inherit genetically from your parents and what you experience environmentally, especially in your early months, determines who you are and how you behave. Determinism it is called.

We know there is enough truth to determinism to take it seriously. But what are the implications? That a person is not responsible for the way he or she behaves? Let us take an extreme illustration of this viewpoint from David Cook's Blind Alley Beliefs.

The kind of thing that illustrates what sociologists have to say would be the story of an Irishman who had a shock of red hair, wore glasses, was 5'11", with a muscular sort of build. He was a highly intelligent fellow Celt. One day he was brutally murdered. It was really a tragic affair. He was carrying a bundle of philosophy of science books because he taught philosophy of science at a college. He happened to see a student that he knew and realizing this student was very interested in the subject, he offered a book to him. Suddenly the student went berserk, and with a couple of karate chops, the lecturer was felled to the ground and died. If they had asked me if I would have a word with the student, I might have uncovered some unusually tragic circumstances. This poor student was brought up in the slums of Liverpool. He lived in a particularly deprived area, and this had left scars on his personality which had affected the whole of his life. Even worse than that was his home background. His father was a highly intelligent man whose real interest in life was philosophy of science. He used to collect books on the subject. Everywhere in his house were philosophy of science volumes. He hardly ever read them, he only collected them, so the house was overflowing with these academic books. The father was an amazing man. He was about 5'11", wore glasses, and sprouted a wild shock of red hair. He was also Irish. In fact, he looked exactly like the lecturer in philosophy of science. We can imagine the situation. Here was a boy brought up in the slums of Liverpool. His father was a mad Irishman, interested in collecting philosophy of science books. The father was also a violent man. His son was always getting into trouble for which his father used to beat him. He would pick up the thing which was nearest to hand in the house (and of course that was a philosophy of science textbook) and lay about his unfortunate child. Day after day, week after week, year after year the son was brutalized by his redhaired, 5'11", muscular Irish father with philosophy of science textbooks. The father had long been in prison for a variety of offences during which time the boy grew up and did very well for himself, and had gone to college. On this particular day, there he was, wandering alone on the campus in the semidarkness of the main building when suddenly a figure emerged from the murky gloom. It was a man. He was 5'11", had an Irish accent, red hair, and in his hand held what looked like a philosophy of science textbook. Of course the boy went berserk and set about the man. Can we blame that boy for what he did? Many today would argue that he was entirely a victim of his social circumstances. He was psychologically and socially conditioned by the terrible experiences he had lived through as a young boy. There should be no question of sending him to prison. He was not guilty of murder. He was not responsible for his actions. What he required was sympathetic understanding, medical treatment and help to come to terms with these terrible social experiences. In other words, in a very real sense he is just like a machine, but a machine gone drastically wrong.[1]

In a lighter vein one psychiatrist wrote this little ditty as a parody on the position of the determinists. It is called "Determinism Revisited." It goes like this:

> I went to my psychiatrist
> To be psychoanalyzed
> To find out why I killed the cat
>   and blacked my wifie's eyes.
> He laid me on a downy couch
>   to see what he could find,
> And this is what he dredged up
>   from my sub-conscious mind.
> When I was one my mommy
>   locked my dolly in the trunk,
> And so it follows naturally
>   that I am always drunk.

> When I was two I saw my father
>   kiss the maid one day,
> And that is why I suffer now
>   from klep-to-man-i-a.
> When I was three I suffered
>   from ambivalence towards my brothers,
> And that is just the reason
>   why I poisoned all my lovers.
> And I'm so glad since I have learned
>   the lesson I've been taught
> That everything I do that's wrong
>   is someone else's fault.[2]

And there's a little chorus that follows:

> Hey, libido, bats in the belfry
> Jolly old Sigmund Freud.

Instinctively we grasp that if people are thus programmed they can't be held responsible. Their response in "the present" is all locked up in their inheritance from "the past." Therefore, they should carry no moral condemnation or affirmation for their present behavior.

By the same token the whole question of who will come to faith, and who will not, seems to have nothing to do with their supposed encounter with the truth. Faith, as it is called, is more a response to the buried and hidden factors of the past than it is to an objective mental assessment of evidence which has been presented for consideration.

And into the quilt goes one more patch of agnosticism, for who can ever know and perceive the truth about anything?

Confusion in the Church

So at church on Sunday morning it's no wonder you find benign confusion in the minds of worshipers. Though they know what their Christian orthodoxy teaches, they have severe doubts about it all. It seems so unfair for God to hold anyone accountable. Surely a God of love and perfect understanding would not reject anyone, especially when they couldn't help themselves because their responses were predetermined by circumstances beyond their control.

And if he will not reject anyone why should I go through the unbelievable personal anguish and risk of rejection from others by trying to convince them to believe in Jesus Christ? They'll be all right in the end, won't they?

So you can see how, by a series of little steps, Christians compromise their position and end up with a vague wishy-washy pabulum that no one can enthusiastically swallow. In vain the minister tries to drum up enthusiastic participation. In vain the few involved laypeople try to encourage others to get involved. Church attendance is average, the singing is poor, the program participation mediocre, and the financial support miserable.

Meanwhile the churches meet in their synods and convocations. They mastermind programs to change the world. Occasionally they make headlines when they vote on something the media deems radically controversial. But it's all a storm in a teacup when viewed realistically. Why? Because you cannot commit to vagaries.

It is only commitment to Jesus Christ and his gospel that will bring life to the church. Anything else is feeding off the limited resources of even the most gifted leadership. Sooner or later they move on or wear out, whether ordained or lay.

Degrees of Agnosticism

Now it needs to be recognized that there are several degrees of agnosticism. Not all agnostics are the same kind of agnostic. Indeed there is a wide range of agnostic expression. It spreads the range from kinship to atheism to profession of Christian faith.

The Committed Agnostic

At one end of the spectrum there is a minority who not only say "I don't know" what to believe about God, but are committed to not knowing. Their a priori position is that you cannot know. For them there is no wistful longing for assurance about God or truth. The one thing they are sure of is that you cannot know God, and there is no way to know the truth about God even if he exists. Their philosophic premise and the foundation stone of their thinking is that one can never know.

On one occasion I stood on the fringe of a group of students in serious discussion about Christianity. One student persistently raised the question, "Where are you coming from when you say that?" He asked it of one student, then another as the discussion continued. After a while I asked him where he was coming from when he asked his question. His answer was, "I don't know."

"How do you know you don't know?" I asked him.

"I don't know that I don't know," he said.

"How do you know that you don't know you don't know?"

"I don't know that I don't know that I don't know."

The young man was a committed agnostic. The absurdity contained both in the conversation and its implications has led many to say the whole world is not only without meaning, it is irrational. "The theater of the absurd" is the expression given to this extreme position by the performing arts, just as on canvas artists try to convey the meaningless chaos of the total agnostic, and many major orchestral works are not a symphony but a cacophony.

The Beatles in the late 1960s and early 1970s popularized this "non-meaning" in a remarkable way. For instance: in "Strawberry Fields Forever" they talked about nothing being real, and living with their eyes closed, yet misunderstanding everything they saw. The title, "Strawberry Fields Forever," recurs throughout the song and is an absolute non sequitur to the lines that precede it.

The total "nonsense" lyric was further enforced by three minutes of recorded music played backwards. I heard one disc jockey in Philadelphia make the rash statement after airing "Strawberry Fields Forever," "Well, that's the end of the Beatles." He further registered disdain at the completely meaningless content and said it was just as well they were finished. But how wrong he was. They continued to publish, and the world at large continued to absorb songs with lyrics that made as little sense. A vast world of young and intelligent people knew exactly what was being said.

Perhaps the ultimate expression of this stream of non-meaning is that of the linguistic philosopher who has reduced all verbal or written language to virtual irrelevance. Consequently there is no such thing as propositional verbal truth to their minds. This is how their argument goes. What you perceive in your mind in the first place is totally subjective; you then take that subjective personal view and describe it in words; those words are communicated to another mind which not only has a totally different understanding of the words but hears them in the context of a totally different life experience. Given this process, they say, there is no objective meaning that can be communicated or understood. If you hold the views of the linguistic philosopher, any conversation at all about God is impossible. The consequences—confirmed agnosticism.

But this is an extreme point of view. Most people are aware of it but do not take it too seriously, for if they did there would be no surviving.

C. S. Lewis, one of the century's most significant communicators of the Christian faith, was at one time an atheist bordering on this level of pessimism. The reasoning process which was part of his coming to faith concluded that if the world was irrational no one would ever know it. They would be part of the whole irrationality. To say anything is irrational is a rational statement. He saw the great contradiction of saying that the one thing that makes sense is that everything is irrational and without meaning. C. S. Lewis rejected the arrogance of such a position and, with the help of a small cadre of professors at Oxford (including Tolkien) who just happened to be Christians, he groped his way to the joy of faith in Christ and a real world filled with truth and meaning.

As you read you may wonder why I refer extensively to the atheistic point of view. Well, it's primarily because atheistic thinking feeds the agnostic mind-set. In all practicality there is no difference between the atheist and the hardcore agnostic. In fact at the height of the agnostic debate in 1880, the Saturday Review of June 26 had these words: "In nine cases out of ten, agnosticism is but old atheism 'writ large.'" If you are convinced and committed to the proposition that "you cannot know God," you have to live as though there were no God. And without question, hardcore agnostics live as though there were "no God." The reason they call themselves agnostic is simply that to say one is an atheist is a statement of faith and carries every bit as much conviction as saying one is a Christian. Agnostics by definition cannot make such a statement of faith.

Well-meaning Agnostics

There is another group we can call "well-meaning agnostics." They are not committed to not knowing. They are by no means pessimistic, nothing-is-real people. They do not go around asking themselves the one meaningful question of the hard-core agnostic, "Why shouldn't I commit suicide?" They think the theater of the absurd is ridiculous and take no pleasure in two tramps waiting on a station platform for someone to arrive who never does, and in the end there is real question as to whether he ever existed. They would never claim to be the brave and authentic person who epitomized the "existential dialectic" who lived in a world without meaning as if it had meaning.

But nevertheless they come close to this last description. The only real difference? It's not out of courage but out of cowardice that they invent for themselves a world of meaning and something for which to live. Otherwise they could not function, let alone survive. In their reflective moments they ask themselves "What for?" but never linger long enough to answer.

Without question, most Americans fall into this category. This is the man and woman on the street. They have a good education, hold good jobs, and invest in leisure very heavily. They make the economy work. They have a sense of what is right or wrong, but not so much so that they would become campaigners. They support the United Way and go to church at Easter and Christmas. They are uncomfortable with their adolescent kids sleeping around but don't want to make it an issue over which to fight, at least not for long.

Here is your liberal, well-rounded, has-a-practical-reason-for-which-he-drifts-with-the-popular-view-of-things person; he can hold a reasonable conversation with the best on a broad range of subjects; pays taxes; doesn't want the world to end with the bomb; desires a good education for the children and sympathizes with, but can't buy into, their dropout mentality. Actually, he wouldn't half mind living in Colorado or New Mexico with them, but being practical he wonders who will pay the bills.

He thinks it reasonable that women should have a "choice" and have equal rights along with homosexuals and other minorities, but will do nothing about their causes and is a little uncomfortable in their presence. This is the man who buys a newspaper daily, invests in the system, and holds season tickets for the Steelers or the Jets, or wishes he did. His wife might be involved in the PTA if she doesn't work, or even if she does. She has begun to find an identity outside the home and would have an abortion if she again got pregnant.

They think their family life should be more meaningful but don't know how to make it so. They have an ambivalent attitude toward the rat race that has produced their success, embracing their activity for the meaning it gives, and loving it for the rewards it offers, but all the while thinking there must be another way. But which way? Who knows? They don't! And so they go on.

Occasionally they hear of a friend's marriage breaking up, and wonder about their own. Drinking has become too important to their life-style but they don't know what to do. They struggle with their weight and have tried one or two of the diets and tried to keep fit, but wonder if it's all worth the effort.

It all goes on and on and there's not much more to say, at least from their point of view. For outside the foci of family, work, and pleasure there is no guiding inspiration to give direction.

The Christian Agnostic

The Christian agnostic is the person for whom this book is primarily written. The expression carries an inherent contradiction of terms. It is precisely this contradiction which describes so well the inner conflict felt by those who are trying to hold together two worlds of thought. They live in both worlds which are mutually exclusive. Indeed they are mutually destructive, and the silent war goes on within the person who cannot let either thought go or give one the authority over the other in his thinking. And make no mistake about it, there is a real warfare here—a real battle for supremacy.

For the Christian agnostic holds in tension the world of the well-meaning agnostic, just described, with the world of the practicing Christian. So he will say grace at meals, at least on major occasions such as Thanksgiving or Christmas when the family gathers for the traditional feast. Prayer plays some part in life along with reading the Bible. He or she serves in leadership in the church, or has done so, and both husband and wife have taken their turn teaching Sunday school. They want their children, as well as others', to get some religious and moral training.

It would be true of many that they even encourage their friends and acquaintances to go to church if the opportunity presents itself. They are quite proud, in a happy way, to be identified with their church and want others to join. They endeavor to come close to "significant giving" and may even call it tithing, though it would not be the traditional 10 percent even after taxes.

The Christian agnostic wants his church to succeed. He doesn't like the general decline in attendance. He is irritated by the pronouncements of church leaders which make the newspaper headlines and also seem to make it all the more difficult to get friends to take the church seriously.

He wishes his minister were a better preacher so that more people might want to attend church. Yet he respects him for who he is and recognizes that every person who enters the rank of the clergy can't be a gifted communicator. For some, this is even viewed as a strength, for they are a little suspicious of the golden-tongued orator. Elmer Gantry still looms large! They don't want their church to become a personality cult around their pastor. After all, you go to church to worship the Lord, not adore the preacher. And yet they still wish there were more life about the place, and might even run the risk of a dynamic preacher if one were to be available at "the right time."

The right time would have to be when their rector was "called" to another parish. As well-intentioned church members it would be viewed as really unchristian to suggest to that minister that he move along. It would hurt him deeply and divide the congregation if word of the suggested leaving ever got out. So the church hobbles along in mediocrity, claiming as its strength its tradition, or wonderful liturgy, or music, or sanctuary, or history, or . . . And the

Christian agnostic hangs in there, discouraged, but in some way part of the team.

The odds seem stacked in this quiet internal battle against the Christian end of the tug-of-war. For even though the Christian agnostic is genuinely religious, he is far from convinced that the Christian faith is for everyone. There is, for instance, an intense dislike for the word evangelism, not just because of the flamboyant style of many well-known TV evangelists but because it implies there are people who really need to be evangelized. All his agnostic, existential, relativistic hackles rise as the strong claims of the Christian faith are made plain. There is insistent confirmation of doubt, and incipient affirmation of faith.

The Searching Agnostic

Everyone must go through a period of "not knowing," since this is a normal step in the process of education. We gather facts, assimilate them, and so come to knowledge. We don't come ready-made with all knowledge. Watching a little child—curious and always learning, never still except when sleeping, constantly in motion, reaching out after the next unexplored opportunity for danger, every waking moment an invitation to adventure—demonstrates the human instinct and desire for knowledge. It is cause for great sadness that life's experience has deadened in so many the questing, searching spirit.

It is precisely this search that Jesus has promised to reward.

"Ask, and it will be given you; seek, and you will find; knock, and it will be opened to you. For every one who asks receives, and he who seeks finds, and to him who knocks it will be opened" (Matt. 7:7-8).

There is the interesting reference in John 1:31 and 33, where John the Baptist twice claimed for himself a kind of agnosticism: "I myself did not know him." But once he received the evidence of who Jesus was he went on to say, "I have seen and borne witness that this is the Son of God" (John 1:34). He moved from ignorance, if you will, to knowledge via a process.

It is in this sense that every convinced Christian was once agnostic. At the beginning he did not know the facts nor did he understand them. Each must tell his or her own story, but one thing is for sure, nearly every Christian came along the difficult pathway of search, struggling through the profusion of data and its confusion of meaning.

It is a process which cannot be short-circuited. Nor can it be stereotyped. We each go through our own personal search. For some it is short and simple; for others long and tortuous. I knew of a man training for the Christian ministry who had tried virtually everything else first—Buddhism, Taoism, Communism, etc. Very few people come to faith easily. Some may seem to, but behind the scenes there has been a praying mother, brother, or friend. It may have been a thought passed on by an associate, a book read, or a painful circumstance gone through. But whatever the input, the struggle and the search went on quietly until the moment of conviction was realized.

The Search for Truth

There are three factors involved in the process of our search for truth.

First, Christianity is not only a "head trip." While the mind is a powerful and important tool in coming to faith, God uses many other avenues of the human experience to bring us to the knowledge of himself. I think of one man who, through the guilt of unfaithfulness to his wife and the desire to save his marriage and family, became a Christian. His wife had already sought her way to a living faith and was the means by which the husband followed suit.

Second, God is very much involved in the process. It is not the case that he is hidden and we have to discover him. On the contrary, if you are a searching agnostic, take heart!

There is a powerful and living God searching for you. The experience is almost universal, when the searcher, having believed, looks back over his journey he sees the Lord has been dogging his steps.

The Bible picture is not that of Little Bo-Peep who "lost her sheep and didn't know where to find him, [leaving] him alone and he'll come home, wagging his tail behind him." No! Jesus portrays God as a shepherd searching for the one lost sheep "until he finds it."

Third, and something we will deal with in a later chapter, is the relationship between fact and faith, or between knowing about God and knowing him personally. Suffice it to say that when we talk about discovering God we are not simply referring to the gathering of data but rather coming into a personal experience which we call "the knowledge of God."

For Reflection and Discussion

1. Which of these categories best fits you?
   a. committed agnostic
   b. well-meaning agnostic
   c. Christian agnostic
   d. searching agnostic
2. Can you remember switching from one position to another?
3. If so, what caused you to change?
4. To which group do you think most of your friends and associates belong?
5. What single factor would be most influential in changing you or your friends to searching agnostics?
6. Do you think there is generally a confusion between knowing about God and knowing him personally?
7. Do you think you would need every question about God resolved in order to know him personally?

3

The Psychology of Agnosticism

There is a myth that most Christians believe and which I want to dispel. It goes like this: People don't believe in Jesus Christ because there are things they don't understand or because there are contradictions in Christianity that remain unresolved.

Now, of course, there are real questions, some of which are very difficult, such as: "Why is there so much suffering in the world?" and "How can a good God allow so much evil?" Such questions are very often asked in the face of personal tragedy. When you lose a child or a husband to cancer, or a son in a road accident, killed by a drunken driver who ought to have lost his driver's license years ago, you may angrily ask, "How can there be a God who would allow this?" We all know people who have suffered such tragedies. I remember a friend going to the hospital each day to see her daughter who was dying of a brain tumor. She passed a part of town where prostitutes waited for business. "Why should my lovely girl be suffering and not one of them?" was her question.

When you add the contradictions between what the Bible teaches and the way most Christians live, the church and the Christian faith become a sitting target for derision. Who could ever believe us? So it goes on. I won't list every kind of question with which all of us are familiar and which shoot down the earnest Christian trying to offer some word of encouragement even before he has hardly begun.

Now please note that I really do admit to the significance of these questions. They need to be answered. But in this section I want to deal with the psychological reasons why many people choose to remain agnostic, and more than that, who look for every shred of kindling to throw on their fire of doubt and confusion. As we have seen they don't have to look very far.

But the reasons they give for their uncertainty about God are not the real issue. Rather, they use real intellectual problems as a smoke screen to protect themselves psychologically against a real faith. There are behind the scenes reasons, sometimes simple, sometimes profound, which are the real reasons why they have chosen to be agnostic and why they work very hard at supporting their agnostic confusion. This then is the myth we need to see through—the myth that there is an intellectual or moral problem with the way Christianity presents itself, when in fact the issue runs closer to the bone, closer to the heart, and has much more to do with who the person is rather than what he says.

I Don't Want to Be Right

At first it may sound very strange to say, "I don't want to be right." Let me state it another way. There is today an aversion to saying someone else is "wrong." It sounds judgmental to say someone else is wrong, especially in the arena of morals or religion. Therefore, by the same token it sounds arrogant to say, "I am right," because if I say I am right it implies all who disagree with me are wrong. "Who am I to say I am right and they are wrong? Far be it from me to stand in judgment on someone else's point of view." So we repudiate and reject any notion that we are indeed right.

But why is this? Surely, you say, we want to be right; we want the truth. Well, in today's climate, in the U.S.A. at least, this is not so, and generally speaking the rest of the Western world is the same. In the Western world it is the "open" mind that appears so attractive in contrast to the "narrow" or "closed" mind which is made to appear so unattractive.

> The spirit of our age is very unfriendly towards dogmatic people. Folk whose opinions are clearly formulated and strongly held are not popular. A person of conviction, however intelligent, sincere and humble he may be, will be fortunate if he escapes the charge of being a bigot. Nowadays the really great mind is thought to be both broad and open— broad enough to absorb every fresh idea which is presented to it, and open enough to go on doing so ad infinitum.[1]

The spirit of anti-dogmatism has been growing for the last fifty years. On May 4, 1940, Dorothy Sayers gave an address in Derby, England. Bear in mind that when she spoke, England had already been at war with Germany for nearly a year. Her address was entitled "Creed or Chaos?"

> The word dogma is unpopular, and that is why I have used it. It is our own distrust of dogma that is handicapping us in the struggle. The immense spiritual strength of our opponents (Germany) lies precisely in the fact that they have fervently embraced, and hold with a fanatical fervor, a dogma which is nonetheless a dogma for being called an "ideology." We on our side have been trying for centuries to hold a particular standard of ethical values which derives from Christian dogma, while gradually dispensing with the very dogma which is the sole rational foundation for those values.[2]

Later in her address she quotes Dr. Selbie, a former principal of Mansfield College, Oxford: "The tragedy is that all this, however interesting to theologians, is hopelessly irrelevant to the life and thought of the average man."

D. L. Sayers responded:

> If Christian ministers really believe it is only an intellectual
> game for theologians and has no bearing upon human life,
> it is no wonder that their congregations are ignorant, bored
> and bewildered.
>   It is not true at all that dogma is "hopelessly irrelevant"
> to the life and thought of the average man. What is true is
> that ministers of the Christian religion often assert that it
> is, present it for consideration as though it were, and, in
> fact, by their faulty exposition of it make it so.[3]

The American equivalent of this discussion is captured
in the statement popular some twenty-five years ago,
"Prayer unites, doctrine divides."

Narrow-mindedness

No one wants to be seen as a narrow-minded bigot. Immediately there comes to mind the tight-mouthed, thin-
lipped image: angry at the world, unloving, unloved, self-
righteous, always condemning, with never a positive word
to say to anyone. It is so easy to caricature this style. We
have all met the withering, judgmental spirit and have come
under its condemnation.

Or, we have met people who seem anachronistic, quaint,
living in a time gone by with an outdated style and values
which are severely in question. Who would want to be
thought old-fashioned? Or, who would want to be written
off as a reactionary or even a "red-neck"? Who on earth
would want to be seen as living in a joyless ghetto of anti-
intellectualism, closing out all the light and truth of fresh
new ways?

Open-mindedness

How much more attractive to be open-minded! There is
a kind of intellectual savoir faire associated with being on
the leading edge of the latest thinking. It's where all the

bright people are who seem so successful and affluent and well-rounded. Better to be thought intelligent and reasonable, even if we are not! Better to be seen as generous in spirit, gracious in attitude, impartial in judgment, wise in disposition. Psychologically you would have to be more drawn to the broad style of the open-minded, especially when you can indirectly add virtue to its list of qualities, the virtue of a modesty which refuses to assert that "I am right," and a humility which says, "Who am I to sit in judgment on your point of view?"

Sociological Experience

There is a powerful sociological reason why this broad-mindedness has been so compatible with the mood of the U.S.A. in the last quarter of a century. Following the Second World War, the fifties witnessed the most amazing boom in the U.S. economy. Hand in glove with its newly experienced wealth came the building of new suburban communities. Families with upward mobility also moved outward to the suburbs. The boom in the economy was matched by a boom in the youth population. Large new high schools and then new and expanded universities were developed. This was also the era of the shopping center to meet the needs of large population transplants.

The common sociological factor in these concurrent movements was the coming together in a new proximity of many varied ethnic and religious backgrounds which hitherto had lived in their own insulated neighborhood. The Second World War of course had begun this process for those who were enlisted in the armed services. Now it moved ahead apace in general.

Parents obviously wanted to begin again in their new communities with their new young families. But it was at the college level where students shared dormitories and screamed support for their college teams that new alle-

giances were formed, which finally superseded the old ethnic backgrounds from which their parents had come.

These students, the majority of whom were being
granted an educational opportunity that their parents never
had, were a strong influence in the movement to submerge
all differences which had fed the old bigotries. Catholics
became less catholic, Protestants less protestant, and Jews
less Jewish. "The Fatherhood of God and the brotherhood
of man" was the catch phrase. It was positively most "un-
cool" to make racial comments, and to "put down" someone else for their religious beliefs. This submerging of distinctions, this ultimate melting-pot experience which carried so much good with it and out of which came the white
support for the civil rights movement of the sixties, provided sociologically the impetus toward new agnostic
mores.

It was during this time that Madalyn Murray O'Hair cam-
paigned successfully to have prayer and Bible reading removed from the schools. Meanwhile, freshmen at universities were going through their Philosophy 101 and learning that you can't be sure of all your old values anymore
and were swept off their moral and spiritual feet by the influence of existential relativistic teachers.

Even the church came to the aid of the movement. With
Bishop John Robinson's book Honest to God, 1963, Harvey
Cox's The Secular City, 1965, and Joseph F. Fletcher's book
on situation ethics in 1966, it became unfashionable to make
clear distinctions and, all overnight, very unacceptable to
stand for a simple "right is right and wrong is wrong" for
fear of being socially obsolete.

The Performing Arts React

Of course, one movement provides the basis for reaction
by the next, and it is interesting to see what form the reaction took. First Archie Bunker came on TV and began to
say out loud all the obnoxious and bigoted things that had

been suppressed for so long, and we all laughed at ourselves. It was a kind of cathartic release of all the pent-up attitudes which for so long had not been allowed free expression. The Jeffersons provided, to some extent, the same opportunity for the blacks. But it was the search for "roots" that marked the longing for a distinctive knowledge of who one was. Alex Haley's book Roots, 1977—a black man's search for identity—popularized on television, was paced by Holocaust, the vivid story of the Nazi extermination of six million Jews. The Jews found a new dignity as they identified with those of their race who were destroyed at Auschwitz or Dachau.

There followed a movement of heightened ethnic distinctiveness. Italians were proud to be Italian. Witness Rocky I, II, and III. Poles were proud to be Polish, especially when the new pope was Polish and Lech Walesa led Solidarnos. In Pittsburgh, where I now live, the fifties had seen the renaissance of the downtown, and it primarily took the form of demolishing much of what is now the Golden Triangle, where the mighty Ohio River begins with the confluence of the Monongahela and Allegheny rivers, and rebuilding it with large office buildings. But, 1980 saw the birth of Renaissance II, and this has been primarily directed at the redevelopment of ethnic neighborhoods, of which Pittsburgh has many.

Religious Reaction

In the spiritual world a similar movement took place. On the negative side there was the growth of the various cults. In amazement and shock, parents who had given their children an affluent home and a fine education watched helplessly as they were drawn into Hare Krishna, the Moonies, Scientology, etc.

In the realm of orthodoxy you had national attention drawn to being "born again," and the tremendous invasion of the "electronic church" into the TV medium.

Meanwhile, the mainline churches which had drifted with the culture in the obliteration of moral and spiritual distinctiveness saw the steady decline of attendance and membership. The opposite was true for those churches, mainline as well as independent, which made plain the claims of Christ. Most of them more than held their own, and there was steady growth in general and in some places extraordinary expansion.

It is apparent that out of the quagmire created by the psychological evasion of "far be it from me to say I am right and you are wrong" has grown a fresh awareness of other, deeper needs. Those needs were insistent and would not be suppressed. Against the unattractiveness of being thought narrow and dogmatic there was the attraction of finding:

1. A sense of distinctive personal identity
2. Psychological satisfaction of commitment
3. Personal fulfillment in belonging.

For such a gain many thought it well worth the risk involved.

This book and this chapter in particular are meant to encourage many more to take that risk. In my conversation and counseling with Episcopalians as well as literally hundreds from the mainline churches—Roman Catholic, Presbyterian, Methodist, etc., it is plain they want to believe, want to be sure of what they believe, and want to be, therefore, people of conviction. Keep going, for you are on to something good!

I Don't Want to Be Intimate

Very few people will tell you outright that they are intimidated by closeness. Some of the people most threatened by intimacy are warm and gregarious at a superficial level. They can chat and laugh and be very embracing in their personality style, but you never get close to them and they don't want you to. So we are not talking about a frigid personality style. We are talking about a wide range of personality styles which are mere facades behind which folks choose to live, sometimes in utter aloneness.

Husbands and wives, no matter how happily married, struggle with genuine intimacy. It's almost as if their lives are three simultaneous dramas. There is the drama which by mutual agreement is the one they act out together; but behind curtains, on two other and separate stages, they each live out their own private drama.

Loneliness is a tremendous problem to the adolescent as well. One of the saddest songs of modern times was written by John Lennon. It's called "She's Leaving Home." It's about the teenage girl who runs off with a truck driver. She slips out of the house at night after her parents have gone to bed. And the song says of her, "She's leaving home, after living alone for so many years." How many young people do you think that describes?

Substitutes for Intimacy

Our modern-day style of life offers a remarkably diverse range of opportunities to "live alone." Private transportation with a CB radio for company, "drive-thru" fast-food services, television viewing that destroys conversation and recreation and offers in turn, especially through the "soaps," a wholly imagined world in which viewers live as though it were real, a drama of substituted intimacy. The most recent phenomenon is of young people encapsulated between earphones closing out the world around them.

Promiscuity and pornography are similar substitutes. Both fulfill the pleasure of sex and give a spurious and surrogate intimacy that denies and abuses the very nature of personhood.

In recent years we have had the advent of computerized bank-telling and pay-by-phone. You even hear commercials where the banking machine carries on a conversation with the customer.

In this same vein, electronic games provide a private world of competition. One wife told me of her husband who, as if TV sports were not enough, bought himself an electronic game to fill up yet more time in isolation with an impersonal screen.

I heard recently of an enterprising group of students in California who offered their services just to listen to problems. They did not counsel or offer advice; they just listened. The need was such for their non-professional, non-involved "ear," that these students were able to pay their way through college on the proceeds.

Alcohol is used to produce a superficial freedom and warmth in company. Many men and women can't even begin to be friendly until they have "had a couple." But at the cocktail party everyone knows it's not for real.

Psychological Nakedness?

It is not that we are advocating a total psychological denuding of one's personhood for the whole world to see who we are. One of the great gifts of humanness is the place of private reflection within ourselves where we can "gather our thoughts," as we say. From a Christian point of view it is within the realm of this inner person that God really goes to work.

And this is precisely the problem for many which causes them to find any excuse not to "engage" spiritually. They realize that at its very center Christian faith is intimacy with God. Intimacy implies vulnerability. Vulnerability implies admission of weakness. Weakness implies admission of inadequacy. Inadequacy implies admission of need. Need implies dependency, and dependency implies the need for intimacy. And so we have come full circle, for dependency is also what faith is all about.

The great fear, even behind the display of the successful "hail fellow, well met," gregarious and sociable person, is, Where will this intimacy end? It's like the trickle through the dam that in the end breaks the whole dam out. The thought is appalling, and very quickly, like the little Dutch boy, they stick their finger in the dike.

But obviously no one is going to say, "I don't want to be intimate because I don't want to be vulnerable." The finger in the dike becomes something like "Christianity is a crutch," or "It seems wrong of God to demand I worship him," or "My faith is personal to me and I don't want to talk about it," or "I'm not the religious type," or "I'm closer to God on the golf course, in the garden, or out in a field," or "Believing in Christ is an admission of weakness." So we find religious alternatives to intimacy.

One of the great attractions of Eastern mysticism or transcendental meditation is the "journey inward." For God then is not a person you relate to. The mantra is not intelligent conversation. You can't converse with a god who is not a person. The focus of such a religion is withdrawal, not engagement; self-searching, not God-searching; getting into oneself, not adoration of God. Once you have said that God is in everything and that he is the sum total of all that is, both of which sound very Christian, you are off the hook in terms of any personal dealings with him or obligation to him.

The temptation is ever present even in the Christian church to avoid intimacy with the living God. That is, to be religious and not spiritual, to foster churchianity rather than Christianity. It is more than interesting that Bishop John A. T. Robinson in his book Honest to God, frankly admitted that prayer for him while at theological college and training for the ministry was not part of his experience, and, apparently, neither was it at the time of writing Honest to God.

And then, equally, there are certain other things that have not rung the bell, certain areas of traditional Christian expression—devotional and practical—which have evidently meant a great deal for most people but which have simply left one cold. The obvious conclusion is that this is due to one's own spiritual inadequacy. And there is clearly a very large amount of truth in this. But I have not forgotten the relief with which twenty years ago, back at my theological college, I discovered in a conversation of the small hours a kindred spirit, to whom also the whole of the teaching we had received on prayer (as it happened to be in this case) meant equally little. There is nothing about it one could say was wrong. Indeed, it was an impressive roundabout: but one was simply not on it—and, what was worse, had no particular urge to be.[4]

Later in his chapter "Reluctant Revolution," he makes an even more amazing claim, given his antipathy to "traditional Christian expression—devotional and practical."

I never seriously thought of being anything but a parson; and however much I find myself instinctively radical in things theological, I belong to the "once born," rather than the "twice born" type. I have never doubted the fundamental truth of the Christian faith—though I have constantly found myself questioning its expression.[5]

All this presumably because he was "born into the heart of the ecclesiastical establishment—the precinct of Canterbury."

It is no wonder that his book Honest to God has as one of its major premises a God who is described in such impersonal terms as "the ground of our being," a phrase he borrowed from Tillich (The Shaking of the Foundations, p. 63). I believe, incidentally, that these biographical insights given by Bishop Robinson are the very reason he struggled with historic traditional Christianity, and why his "interpretation" of its foundational truths looked more like a "denial." There is a tremendous pathos in the heart as one identifies with the spiritual hunger this circumstance creates, and an anger at the arrogance that allows men of expressed, if not avowed, skepticism to continue in leadership. One admires their courage in being "honest" but wishes their honesty would have led them also to step down from leadership in the church before publishing abroad their doubtfulness.

The obvious hardly needs to be stated: If leaders in the church are so secular in their presentation of the Christian faith, it's no wonder that churchianity rather than Christianity abounds.

Religious Art

The same depersonalization of God occurs in the field of the arts. Christendom is everywhere infiltrated with authorities in the realm of religious art who can tell you what all its symbols represent and from which country and century they come, but who refuse to be intimately acquainted with the God these symbols communicate.

Christian music represents a similar dilemma. Many who love Handel's Messiah do not love the Messiah himself, and remain ambivalent about the possibility. There is more than a sneaking suspicion that the beauty of the liturgy and ritual, and the tradition of the hymns and Sunday morning itself, are enjoyed for themselves rather than the Lord to whom they are meant to lead us.

Our tendency to become impersonal in our religion will never disappear, for our frail humanness is always threatened by genuine intimacy. That is why I love the opening prayer of Holy Communion in the 1928 Book of Common Prayer: "Almighty God, unto whom all hearts are open, all desires known, and from whom no secrets are hid." There is hardly a more appropriate way to enter into prayer and worship, because we acknowledge God's intimate knowledge of us, and in so doing are encouraged to be open toward him.

If you are one who has been granted the grace to move beyond this personal threat of intimacy, make no mistake about it, the Collect for Purity, as it is called, begins where most want to stop. We understand why, for we were once there and once made the step of faith from personal privacy into his presence.

We have also gone through periods of "dryness and distance" in our relationship with God which have further helped us realize the tendency to move from intimacy to formality. So it is, with all fellow travelers, we admit to the problem, but in all humility refuse to surrender to it.

I Don't Want to Be Like Them

Another major factor for people refusing to become thoroughgoing Christians is their extreme distaste at the thought of being like "them."

"Them" may be all sorts of Christians or just one sort. Without question the "Are you saved?" variety is mentioned frequently on the menu of distaste. Then there is the "Praise the Lord" and "raise your hands" in worship group. The media—Christian and secular—love the graphic communication of a large crowd raising their hands. The more retiring churchgoer or skeptical non-churchgoer views with horror the thought of having to express a faith, for which they may secretly long, in such an extroverted and exhibitionist manner.

For others, emotionalism—"ickiness," sentimental slop as they perceive it—revolts their own reserved and private manner. They don't want to be weepy, huggy, kissy. This is the very reason the "peace" was a controversial addition to the 1979 Book of Common Prayer in the Episcopal church. Resistance to it had nothing to do with theology and everything to do with having to touch another person, look him in the eye, and speak a personal word. Why, even the bishops and clergy et al don't just shake hands; they are up there hugging one another! When we want privacy for our own personal thoughts, intimacy legislated by the service seems all the more repugnant.

And yet there are many who are put off by the quiet reserve of churchgoers. I once visited a small church with maybe eighty people in the congregation; not one of those oft criticized large impersonal churches where you get lost in the crowd. I was not dressed as a clergyman and was not known by anyone in the congregation. At the close of the service I stood just outside the only exit from the church with Sarah, our one-year-old baby, in my arms—not a forbidding specter! I looked kindly at each person as they came by me, almost inviting them to speak to me a word of welcome. Not one, not one, spoke. Who would want to become one of them?

And of course, there is church itself! I am personally staggered at how unaware most clergy and church people are of the visitor in their midst who hasn't the faintest idea about what's going on. For your average, reasonably educated, semi-interested but definitely secular person who has found his or her way to church, almost daring God to get through to them and risking one more chance that he may, the church offers God further hurdles over which he must climb.

I was once such a person. For a start I didn't like the smell of old churches—which most are where I was raised in Oxford, England. I enjoyed popular music—which the hymns most definitely were not. No page numbers were announced. Then I had to try to sing the psalm, having found it after the congregation had begun, which had no rhyme, to music which had no meter, from a book which had no music, in Anglican chant which had barely a detectable melody. Well, it was just impossible!

The feeling that I had to become one of those antiquarian folks, and master a service which just wasn't my style or taste, presented one more reason why I should remain uninvolved. To tell the truth, the preaching was the only redeeming event of the service. What if it had been the anticlimax to an otherwise totally uninspiring event! Who would want to be like that?

It's all so very laughable, and yet tragically often the case, that it is this sort of problem, and not the battle for the truth that's going on within a person's mind, that is allowed to become the deterrent to knowing God.

I want to present a dual plea. To the Christians I would say, examine your church through the eyes of the inquiring agnostic who arrives in your pew on Sunday morning, from the moment they step on your property until the moment they leave. Are you giving them an easily-clung-to reason why they should not come back and why they should not take the gospel seriously?

And to those who are claiming to be agnostic and using either the fanatical or the bland Christians as an excuse why they should remain so, please look beyond the quirks and limitations of our human expression. Just as you would not reject the notion of love, marriage, and family because of so many miserable and poor expressions of it, so don't annul the possibility of knowing God because of the poor job we Christians do.

I Don't Want to Be a Hypocrite

"I don't want to be a hypocrite!" How often you hear this as a reason for not going to church! The Christian quickly realizes the oblique and intended criticism. Hypocrisy is perhaps the most devastating accusation against the church. It is a tragedy that our apparent holier-than-thou self-righteousness, with its attendant judgmental attitude, drives away the very people that the Lord Jesus himself would welcome.

It's sort of like a hospital representing itself as antagonized by the sick and injured. Remember the point of rejection of Jesus by the Pharisees, the religious purists of his day? "This man receives sinners and eats with them" (Luke 15:2). What they in their self-righteousness saw as a reason to condemn Jesus has become the very heart of the Christian gospel. Indeed, not only is Jesus waiting for sinners, he is looking for them (see Luke 19:10).

Jesus' definition of hypocrisy was the bragging display of an exterior righteousness which covers up an interior rottenness; the whitewashed tomb was one of his analogies.

Another part of the Bible puts it this way, "If we say we have no sin, we deceive ourselves, and the truth is not in us. If we confess our sins he is faithful and just, and will forgive our sins and cleanse us from all unrighteousness" (1 John 1:8–9). That's why I love the bumper sticker "Christians aren't perfect, just forgiven."

You can understand how, even when Christians aren't self-righteous, they can appear to be so. We are called to be "down" on sin, but we are not to be down on the sinner. Invariably, though, the two are perceived as the same. Doctors and nurses don't love illness and pain. That would be sick and morbid. Their job is to attack disease and suffering as the enemy, but also in the process to care for and support the patient.

Just in passing, note that doctors and nurses get sick too, and when they do they use the same prescription and treatment which they offer. So it is with Christians.

Most of the time, however, while the church stands guilty of hypocrisy, the person who uses hypocrisy as a reason for not going to church is also really making excuses. He or she is involved in lots of other activities and pursuits which are filled with hypocrites. I've never heard anyone say, however, "I don't go to work because the place is full of hypocrites." We all know that there are hypocrites who are managers and hypocrites who are trade unionists, and there are hypocrites who are neither. They are in sports, movies, stores, schools, politics—and church.

If the truth be told, there is a full measure of hypocrisy in the excuse! It's as if the person is saying, "I'm not a hypocrite and I'm not going to become one." All of a sudden he sounds virtuous. That's why some respond to the comment "The church is full of hypocrites," with "There's always room for one more."

On the other hand, some are saying "I'm no good." Their feeling is that the church is for good people and if they go they are pretending to be good, and that's hypocrisy. In a few rare cases this may be a genuine expression, and where it is there is the good news that the church is not for good people but for those who know they need forgiveness.

Most of the time this is just another psychological evasion. In going to church one runs the risk of meeting God. If I am trying to avoid him today, hypocrisy becomes the useful weapon in my hand. It makes the Christian feel guilty while I walk away appearing virtuous.

The average red-blooded American man or woman has an ambivalent love-hate relationship with goodness or righteousness. For certain they are skeptical of anyone who tries to come off as too good. Message oriented advertising is viewed with great cynicism: the steel company that's "involved," the electronics company that "brings good things to living," the car that "you can believe in," or the gasoline company that gives you tips on how to save gas while advertising with the devious intention of luring you to buy more of theirs. What about the petro-chemical company that saved all the ducks!

Nevertheless there is admiration for righteousness that doesn't parade itself, and a longing for goodness in ourselves and families. We want to supplant the jaded skepticism with something closer to naiveté and beauty. Purity and innocence are more sexually alluring than flouncing, bosomy, semi-nudity. It's a sad quirk of the human disposition that we make righteousness appear to be ugly. We abuse the word puritanical, for instance, and make it a derogatory statement about another person. Yet in reality being "pure" should be seen as a desirable virtue and worthy of admiration.

I Don't Want to Change

Change, to anyone who has moved beyond adolescence, is always uncomfortable. Perhaps that's why in the late 1960s we heard the slogan, "Don't trust anyone over 30." One psychologist actually hypothesized that we are adolescent until age thirty. But there is one kind of change that is uncomfortable to all ages and which even the teenager, though addicted to change, finds profoundly disturbing. It's the change called repentance.

The word repentance as variously used in the New Testament means a change of mind, a change of heart, to experience remorse. (See Kittel's Theological Dictionary, vol. 4, p. 626.) The net effect is not just a feeling of sorrow about a mistake made or a sin committed, but a change of mind which results in a change of behavior.

Today there is a general distaste for the word repentance because it sounds judgmental (you've done something wrong), and radical in the sense that it calls for an immediate and thorough change. We don't like to think we have really been wrong, and in any case don't want to be told; nor do we want to change, least of all immediately and thoroughly. Behavior modification we think is more evolutionary from within, via an educational process of enlightened self-interest. We don't want to be told. We would rather discover.

At the real heart of it the issue is moral. It is our response not just to an imperative from within (I feel I should change), but a word of authority from without (Thus saith the Lord).

In the context of our discussion we need to stop and realize that most people when confronted with the Christian message aren't going to say, "I won't believe because it means too many changes. I like the wrong things I am doing too much to give them up."

The more natural psychological ploy is to find fault or ask the kind of questions that foster doubt, and thereby quietly defend a self-centered way of life. I remember spending an evening with a university student who had left home, thrown off the Christian faith and values in which he had been raised, and was living in his own apartment. For two to three hours we discussed many intellectual problems that had recently caused him to doubt the salient truths of his Christian heritage. The routine was very familiar. As soon as I had answered one question, he would raise another, and so it went on all evening. Finally, I said I didn't believe his problem with Christianity had anything to do with the reasons he claimed. Rather, I suggested his problem was a moral one. He wanted to live out with his girlfriend a sexual relationship that was contrary to Christian morals. He just smiled at me. No more words, no more arguments.

The warfare that is being waged behind the intellectual barrage of inquiry is invariably spiritual. The Christian who would be the most help to his or her friends must constantly refresh himself with God's view of what is going on behind the closed doors of human personality.

For instance, I am constantly amazed at how many Christian friends get sidetracked by the criticism aimed at their church or their minister. I am willing to concede that the criticism is valid in my own case, and I strive to improve, where I am able, both the program of the church and my own personal life or ministry. But years of experience have taught me that even after I have put things right, it is only a matter of time before the faultfinders surface again, casting doubt on my integrity and my work. At an experiential level it finally became plain to me what was going on. The problem was the message.

But the Bible's teaching about our spoiled humanity and its pronounced bias to do wrong and not right ought to have given the clue. "For I know that nothing good dwells within me, that is, in my flesh. I can will what is right, but I cannot do it. For I do not do the good I want, but the evil I do not want is what I do" (Rom. 7:18–19). This is the frank admission of the apostle Paul (see also 2 Cor. 10:3–5).

Since I have become a father I have gained a profound understanding of the problem. We have never had to teach our children to do wrong or rehearse them in bad manners. Further, it's amazing how quickly they inhale their parents' failures and resist our refinement.

In our adult world what would you suppose people might be defending by their well-built wall of doubt? Economic success—the love of what money can buy and what it takes to obtain it? Career success—the desire for status and power and what it takes to get to the top? Social success—the acceptance, and even acclaim, of those I want most to admire me? Simple hedonism—addiction to pleasure and the environment and compromise of pleasure seekers? Resentment—the grudge we harbor against someone or some group which has deeply hurt us and which we will not let go?

If you are anything like I am you resist the notion that people are so superficial. You want to credit them with noble intentions. You want to believe that if you could just help your friends resolve their intellectual conflict they would capitulate to the love of God for them. But if you have come to a living faith, look back to the real obstacles which stood before you and your acceptance of the Lord onto the throne of your life. While all of us have reasonable questions which need to be answered concerning the substance of the faith, is it not true that we constantly weigh our response against the changes that have to take place?

In one sense the immediate changes we see standing before us are superficial. They only point to the ultimate "repentance" and, as we weigh them, indicate the need for an "ultimate conversion." For while repentance of individual sins is necessary, it is repentance of the heart's intention and direction that the Christian faith in essence calls for. The rearrangement of the deck furniture was important, but more important was the turning of the boat headed for the Niagara Falls.

I remember as if yesterday an encounter with an educated and cultured man in his middle years. Bob had actually been raised and schooled in the Roman Catholic tradition but had long since ceased to practice his faith. He was president of a small but well-known company, married, and had three children. I had made an appointment to visit with his wife, Marnie, one afternoon, since the family had a loose connection with the church. His curiosity got the better of him and he took the afternoon off so that he could see what the "new chap" was like.

It was an unforgettable encounter. After all the usual small talk, some of which included the business of the church, we came to the matter of what Christians believe, or are supposed to. I think it is true to say that neither of us wasted words, so it was not too long before we reached "the bottom line." Autonomy was the issue. Bob saw that Christian faith was more than what you believe by way of intellectual proposition, and more than how you behave in your manner of life. He cut, like a hot knife through butter, the myriad of details to this one single principle, "Who shall run my life?" Would Jesus Christ be a passenger in the car from whom he sought direction from time to time, or would Jesus Christ be seated behind the wheel—not just the navigator but the driver? If taking that step is perceived as the ultimate repentance, conversion, you immediately see, poses the ultimate threat.

Independence and control are challenged at the fundamental level in the human personality. I shall never forget the experience of riding through the streets of London in a sidecar attached to a motorcycle. The traffic was heavy and London drivers are aggressive. New York, Boston, and Rome have similar champions of the velocipede! I was helpless to direct the motorcycle and as vulnerable as can be, stuck out on the side with only a thin shell between me and constant danger.

Surrender to Jesus Christ seems to offer the same set of dangers to one's life-direction and purpose. Even if we are not doing a particularly good job of running our own show, at least we are in control.

Perhaps the supreme example of the autonomy "issue" is a friend, Jim, who before he retired was a Navy flier, that is, he flew jet planes on and off the deck of an aircraft carrier. In describing what it meant for him to become a Christian, he took us back to a day when he surrendered control of his life to Jesus Christ. All of his life, as a Navy flier, the name of the game was to be in total control of his environment. Using that experience as an illustration, he said that the most difficult thing for him in coming to faith in Christ was surrendering the control of his life-environment to another. He also shared the deep sense of joy and release that came with Jesus Christ as his own personal pilot.

The Cultural Counterflow

I want to reflect briefly on our contemporary scene to observe the cultural counterflow to the Christian faith. The mood today is one of "self-actualization and self-assertion." We are no longer astonished at the immodesty of athletes with arms aloft proclaiming, "We are number one." There is something appealing in the advertisement which says, "Have it your way," and still another one which says, "You

deserve a break today." The "do your own thing" philosophy has produced a "me-istic" generation of young adults
whose influence is so pervasive it seems the rest of the adult
world has followed its lead—even when widowed retirees
are living together out of wedlock it no longer shocks us.
As a general public we are sated with the propaganda of
special interest groups which many believe are endanger-
ing the nature of our political process in Washington. The
extension of the rights movement all the way down to
school age has children seriously questioning the parents'
right to exercise any authority in their lives. One astonished
parent shared with me his resentment that, while he pays
the enormous expense for his son's education, he is not entitled to a school report on his academic process without
the son's permission.

It is plain that the dream once so fondly held that the education of the populace and a fairer distribution of wealth
which would create a society that would live in a spirit of
largess and equanimity, has become a nightmare of self-
centered narcissism. Dallas and its TV counterparts could
not have described the mood more perfectly. The strange
love affair of the public with J. R. was perhaps their admission that their life is seen in terms of "looking after number one."

There is no question in my mind that our culture has driven us back to the biblical conclusion that "the heart is de-
ceitful above all things, and desperately corrupt; who can
understand it?" (Jer. 17:9). For many the claim to be agnostic is a deceit of the heart and an excuse for "doing one's
own thing." That spirit of independence, rather than ac-
complishing personal fulfillment, has reaped a harvest of
arrogant loneliness.

If the nature of sin is properly understood, at its core is
the drive for independence. Plainly, the Garden of Eden
delusion was that in doing his own thing man would be fulfilled, "be as God," and that God in asserting his authority

was "depriving man" of such fulfillment. The history of humankind ever since has not been the search for God, but rather of hiding from God. God has been doing the searching. We have been busy as ever since then picking psychological fig leaves behind which to hide our real selves and our real motivations from each other.

The threat of the change called repentance has produced many such fig leaves. Another friend of mine, by the name of George, said that for him the physical act of kneeling in church symbolized his capitulation and surrender to Christ and was the most difficult thing he had ever done. Of George it can be supremely said that he never bowed the knee to anyone before that moment, and I don't think he's bowed the knee to anyone else ever since.

I Don't Want to Decide

Sir Arthur Bryant, the English historian, said, "There is nothing more destructive of action than a tortured undecided mind."

There is in our present culture a reticence to make hard and fast decisions. Procrastination is a common ailment. It is no small cause of frustration in the home. At work it divides those who drag on in mediocrity from those who succeed. For some, a restaurant menu of any size becomes a major frustration. When the waitress comes to take their order I have heard people say, "Decisions, decisions, decisions." We are all aware of the letters we haven't written, the phone calls we haven't made, the mother we haven't visited, the birthday card we never got around to buying or, worse still, the one we bought but never sent! A scholar friend of mine has a card displayed in his library which says, "National Procrastination Day Has Been Postponed." Presumably an amusing way to say, "Get on with it!"

The Christian faith demands a decision. Most people are vaguely aware that a response must be made and so they shy away, not because they have serious intellectual doubts or even a grave moral problem. They just are not ready to get involved with one more commitment, especially when it is so far-reaching in its ramifications. Since in a sense, not to decide is to decide, I want us to consider some reasons why procrastination or indecisiveness is endemic to our present time.

Tyrannized by the Urgent

Modern life is filled with immediacies and urgencies. These are to be distinguished from what is important. It has been my experience that things of importance get crowded out by lesser but more urgent details. Just to live today is to be deluged with immediacies, car inspections, tires to be changed, expense accounts, tax returns, doctor and dentist appointments, bills to be paid, and children to encourage, discipline, and ferry from one activity to the next. It's shopping, cooking, cleaning, entertaining, weeding, or shoveling snow.

Recreation has become a major industry. The more we own, the more we are owned. And, without prolonging the litany, you are emotionally aware of the plethora of urgencies which crowd and harass you. The consequent weariness militates against making even the most simple decision if it's not essential at the moment.

Pragmatism versus Idealism

At a deeper level, and of more consequence, is the battle between the "pragmatic" and the "ideal." Pragmatism leads to something I can immediately get busy with. Idealism questions the very principles which lie behind my activity. One of the reasons we deliberately crowd our lives with mundane practicalities, or even frenetic recreation, is to defend ourselves against thinking seriously about why we are doing them. Busyness is a comforting alternative to reflectiveness. Without time to reflect there is no fear of my having to make the decision about the weightier matters of the soul. Harry Blamires, in the chapter entitled "The Surrender to Secularism," makes this observation on British pragmatism.

> The English philosophy in this respect is a simple one. If six people disagree violently about where they want to go, the best thing to do is to set them to work making a car so that, in the long run, they can go somewhere, easily and comfortably. Meantime one hopes that something external may occur which will provide an obvious reason for going to one destination rather than another. Or indeed the finished car might, by a lucky fluke, turn out to have a convenient if unforeseen technical bias in its steering which inclines it to turn in one direction rather than another. And until the hour of decision arrives, there is a tacit understanding among the six makers of the car that all reference to its future use will be rigidly excluded from their conversation. They will do their best to compensate for any frustrations on this score by talking fast and furiously about the mechanics of manufacture and the relative merits of various petrols, lubricants, plugs, and batteries.[6]

If this is true of the English, it is true in spades of the American. Our enthusiasm for getting things done makes the British look depressed by contrast.

And yet, "The Hound of Heaven" never lets up. He has chased many a fox across many a field. He knows our evasions. He has seen them all before. In my case it was the word of a man who managed a butcher shop in Oxford, where I grew up. I worked on Friday nights after school helping clean the shop and prepare for Saturday morning. One Friday I missed my work at the butcher shop in order to try out for the school cricket team. On Saturday morning he wanted to know why I didn't tell him I would be absent. I said, "I had intended to tell you." He replied, "The path to hell is paved with good intentions."

Not long after that I met a man, Ray Wilson, who told me of the new life I could experience in Jesus Christ. For three years following, from fifteen to eighteen, I made wily, fox-like moves, but all the time "was pursued." My primary evasion was, "I'll settle this later." And I heard the wisdom of the Oxford butcher, "The path to hell is paved with good intentions."

It was at Harringay Arena in 1954 that I was caught. Billy Graham was then the young preacher who wooed England. I went to hear him and left having chosen Christ. The hunt was over, the procrastination finished, the decision made.

Existential Drift

There has been among the student population of the last few decades, at least, what I will call an existential drift. It's a deadly mixture of relativism, and a narcissistic pre-occupation with fulfillment and pleasure. It has diminished the sense of obligation to parents who have raised them and the institutions which have nurtured them. This has produced an if-it-feels-good-do-it philosophy writ large.

Relatively few really decide to get married. They drift into it via a courtship that has experienced all the intimacies of marriage. It's almost as if the obligation to get married has been incurred and they may as well go through with it.

Tens of thousands have dropped out of school in "search of themselves." Very few of them will have actually made the decision to leave school. Their grades made that decision for them. Dr. Anthony Campolo amusingly has pointed out how many end up "going West to Colorado trying to find themselves." He goes on to say, "Self is not discovered by a search but is made by our choices."

The existential bloom-where-you-grow philosophy has produced only the desire for immediate gratification and withered any sense of destiny and the necessary decisions that go into the pursuit of such a destiny.

Corporate Process

Many of those who made it through their education entered into a corporate world where the company manual determined the style and the regimen of work life. The ones who executed most diligently the company directives and policy were the most likely to succeed. The system and its process has the conditioning effect of minimizing personal judgment and individual decision making. This is terrific for the business, and one can see the potential for chaos if it were run some other way, but I have witnessed its debilitating effect in the lives of too many corporate men and women. They seem unable to make difficult decisions and carry the risk and responsibility that go with them. Since the decision to follow Christ presents obvious risk and difficulty, the problem of becoming a Christian has been magnified.

Church Process

There is a sense in which the "system and process" mindset has also invaded the church. If one aspect of evangelism is calling for a decisive commitment, then it is no wonder so little of it happens in church. I will describe the Episcopal church by way of example, but I am sure nearly all other denominations have the same problem.

The Episcopal process is to get Susie baptized as a baby and to bring her to church and to Sunday school. As she grows older and has more understanding she is admitted to the Communion rail for Holy Eucharist. Then she is confirmed and presumably goes on to be an adult Christian and an Episcopalian. The process is seen in sacramental and educational terms. Presumably the sacraments nurture the soul and education nurtures the mind, and between them they produce a Christian.

Now, of course, as a minister I believe in the Christian sacraments and in Christian education. But neither of these of necessity makes a Christian. The missing ingredient is the call to commitment. It is the decision to commit one's life to Christ that produces virile Christians instead of just process Christians. The church itself is a tremendous mission field because the wills of the people have not been challenged to choose Christ. "Repent and believe," or "Choose you this day whom you will serve" are not topics for discussion, but an address to the will. Being a Christian is a matter of choice. It is not a process like osmosis where, if you sit in the church long enough, something good will happen to you. Neither is it a religious feeling. Christian faith is not merely knowledge of Christian truth; it is a decision made to surrender to Christ.

Fear of upsetting the congregation is a significant problem for the clergy. One of the crying needs in the educational process of the church is the training of Sunday school teachers to lead children to commitment to Christ. A remarkable number of adult Christians today chose Christ as children. While that commitment had to mature along with the rest of their understanding, it was valid and real. Frances Ridley Havergal, the author of such hymns as "Take My Life and Let It Be," "O Saviour, Precious Saviour," and "Lord, Speak to Me That I May Speak," became a Christian as a child. When her Sunday school teacher, whom she loved, said how pleased she was, Frances said, "Yes, miss, but I should have been yours; you should have been the one to bring me to Christ."

It's an emotionally taxing charge, but preachers must challenge the will. I know from experience I would rather talk around and about Christianity. There is a time for Rogerian style counseling. There is a time for listening and absorption. There is a time simply for the "ministry of presence." But sooner or later there must be a time when we ask our friends to choose Christ.

One of the reasons there is such a response to Billy Graham is that so few people have ever been put in the position to "choose you this day whom you will serve." If you are a minister who has hesitated to do this, pray for the courage and take the plunge. The joy of gathering fruit in the vineyard is worth the few sour grapes of rejection.

Weekend conferences and times away are vital, and very productive in this matter of decision making. It is a chance to leave behind the urgent details of daily life and deal with the important matters of eternal life. Get away for such a spell of time and invite your friends to go with you. Have your church arrange a weekend.

For Reflection and Discussion

1. Which psychological evasion do you feel is the most common?
   a. the desire to be open-minded
   b. the threat of intimacy
   c. aversion to religious style
   d. the distaste for hypocrisy
   e. resistance to the profound change from self-reliant to God-reliant
   f. plain old procrastination and the inability to make a firm decision
2. Which could you most easily deal with yourself?
3. Which is the most difficult for you?
4. Which ones are you aware of overcoming?
5. What other psychological evasions can you think of?
6. Do you agree that most people use intellectual arguments as a smoke screen so they do not have to deal with the personal threat that a genuine faith in a personal God presents?
7. List ways in which you might help someone move beyond their particular hang-up.

4

Our Fundamental Options

....

I t is time to examine the three fundamental possibilities which confront us. We do so with the hope that, despite the current cultural predisposition to remain agnostic and indecisive you will find yourself irresistibly drawn to a thorough-going faith in Jesus Christ. While we have discussed many issues surrounding agnosticism, when we get down to the fundamental options there are only three.

1. There is no God.
2. There is a God who has chosen not to reveal himself.
3. There is a God who has chosen to reveal himself.

There Is No God

We begin by acknowledging, once again, that the agnostic refuses to draw the atheistic conclusion, "There is no God." However I want us to look at what this alternative really represents as a view of reality, for many have never pressed it to its practical conclusions, and still flirt with it as a possibility. And that flirtation is part of the agnostic dilemma.

No Designer-No Design

If there is no God, there is no ultimate designer of creation. There being no designer, there is no design. I know you often hear mention of "Mother Nature" as if there is some innate design process that she works out. We have heard a theory of evolution which talks as if "nature" has a mind of its own, so the mutations match need, that is, if a bird needs webbed feet to survive in a watery environment, the force of nature throws up just such a mutation. But in reality it is all one staggering accident initially, followed by millions of equally remarkable accidents. Anything that looks like design is only apparent, if there is no God.

If there is no design because there is no designer, then there is no objective moral right or wrong. That is, there is no ethical design by which human beings ought to live because they were designed that way. Granted we have developed our socio-ethical systems to allow rational creatures to coexist, as suggested, for instance, by J. J. Rousseau who wrote The Social Contract in 1762.

Humanity in its early development credited God with these systems partly because in the primitive mind there really was a God, but also because leaders, in order to give credence to their edicts, made God the author of their rules. But if there is no God, what we call ethics and morals are only an extension of man's rational ingenuity so that people might live peaceably together.

Similarly, conscience, rather than being designed into the human personality by God, is simply developed by the expectations of the family or culture in which we are raised. Even if it seems to be innate, it is only the result of generations of inbreeding so that I somehow have inherited much of my conscience genetically from all that my forebears were becoming.

There is even the view that if we have evolved to be moral beings, then we are meant to act morally, and are morally bound to do so. If you are a moral being, even if you became one by the accidents of nature, you should behave like a moral being.

The secularized Western nations which once believed that moral law came from God, and incorporated such a view into their constitutions (including the U.S.A.), are now going through the most remarkable demonstration of pragmatic, legal, and moral gymnastics, to divest themselves of the top-down, God-ordained code of ethics, while endeavoring to retain some sort of moral foundation on which to base their decisions.

Meanwhile, at the grass roots of our society, people are adopting a highly personalized view of morality. Junior and senior high school students are being educated in the "development of values" for themselves, apparently based on the assumptions that (a) there is no one who can autocratically give them their values, including their parents, and (b) people of good sense, good education, and good intention will develop good values. It is not surprising that we have thus entered into a culture of moral chaos.

But to return to my main theme; if there is no objective moral standard of behavior that is ordained by design from "outside," that is, by a transcendent God, then we are left with the moral corollary of nature's "survival of the fittest," namely, "right by might." Those who determine what is right or wrong are the ones with the power to do so. Here is a straightforward description of reality—the way things are.

Furthermore, we must realize that "right by might" is an amoral description of reality. If there is no God, and therefore no ultimate right or wrong, there is nothing innately wrong with "right by might." We have simply come to an understanding of how, in the absence of moral absolutes, rights or wrongs are determined, that is, how each individual society in order to function organizes itself by its laws, which I have called rights and wrongs.

Significance and Sanctity?

Following another line of thought which stems from the "no-God" view of reality, I want to draw yet another conclusion. There is no more significance or sanctity to being human than there is to being a cow, a tree, or a common housefly. We all got here by the same process. Some of us evolved into cows and others evolved into people. But innately we as humans are no more significant, and our existence is no more sacred. When we die we return to the elements just as does all other living matter. Oh, I know we have given ourselves more significance because we have exceptional intelligence. We can also reflect upon the nature and consequence of our "being" or our "behavior" because we have premeditative and volitional attributes and can therefore hold one another accountable. But our distinctions are arbitrary and obviously from the human point of view. What if we take the housefly's point of view and determine significance by the dual measurements of the complexity of our seeing mechanism or the ability to fly with wings? Or what if we take the ant's point of view, and make it the ratio of weight and size to strength?

If there is no God to give the commandment, "Thou shalt do no murder," what is wrong with killing people? We kill flies, cows, and ants. In any ultimate sense there is no difference. We all came by way of a mindless, amoral evolutionary process, and when we die we shall all return to mindless, amoral matter!

By way of example I want us to take Germany's Third Reich under the rule of Hitler's Nazi party and subject it to the "no God" analysis of reality.

First of all there was nothing wrong with the Nazis killing their political opponents, whether Jew or Christian. Nothing was wrong with killing the insane. Nothing was wrong with experiments on human life, in particular the reproductive process of women. In trying to produce "a super race" and thin out from it anything deemed inferior, Hitler was doing nothing less among humans than the enterprising farmer does with his livestock. Within the terms of our discussion, Hitler's might made him right. It only became wrong when the Allied Forces subdued the Third Reich. Then it was that another might determined what was right.

Had Hitler won the world, his word, backed by his power, would have become law.

I am personally repulsed by this atheistic theory spelled out explicitly in terms of the Third Reich. A similar application could be made to atheistic communism and even in the minds of some skeptics to the Western democracies. It really does appear that "might determines right" and when all is said and done, it is Darwinian Survival of the Fittest among humans as well as the animal kingdom.

In a somewhat sarcastic vein, I remember reading in Punch magazine, about the year 1965, a brief article pleading the Darwinian case against humanity having to behave like anything other than the animal kingdom from which it had come. "Why frustrate me" implied the author, "with all the trappings of moral obligation to behave differently than I desire when my desires are exactly those I have inherited from my animal forebears? If all in nature is 'red in claw and tooth' why try to make humans behave any differently?" he asked. And of course he asks the right question.

But the questions I want to ask you as you read this are, Does the no-God theory match your view of reality? Could you adopt the atheistic position and give it free reign in its application to the whole of life? In addition, when you take into consideration the psychological and emotional hopelessness that goes with a world without God, does it not reinforce the conclusion of the psalmist, "The fool says in his heart, 'There is no God'" (Ps. 14:1)?

The Anonymous God

This viewpoint would suggest there is no God. That is to say, God has not deliberately and with intention declared who he is, what he has created the world to be, what his expectations are of us, and how we can know him personally. Rather, those of this opinion tend to suggest, God made everything and then withdrew, or at least remains hidden and anonymous. We humans are left with the exhilarating challenge of investigating the world he created and determining what God is like from his handiwork.

There are three assumptions commonly held by those who commend to us this "unknown God." First, he is a good God. His attitude toward us is benevolent. If we imitate his benevolence by trying to keep the Golden Rule we shall win his approval.

Second, all religious roads lead up to the mountaintop of God. Each of the religions has discovered a part of the truth in its search for God. None can say it has all the truth or that it is superior to the others. They all began with the same basic ingredient: they could observe the world that had been made by God, and by such observation each determined what God was like. In addition they have deduced what the world was for, how we should live, and how we can draw close to God.

Third, this view adorns God with greatness, declaring that by very definition God would have to be too fast for any single religion to have a monopoly on his time or interest, or to have a monopoly on the truth.

Our anonymous God then, is benevolent, non-discriminating, and vast. All routes, no matter how circuitous, lead to heaven, and therefore all will get there in the end.

An Analogy

I want at this point, by use of a thirst-and-water allegory, to give an interpretation of this popular world life view.

Let us suppose that God created humankind with the physical experience of thirst but never created water to quench it. And, for the sake of our allegory, we imagine that it is possible to exist without water. So from the beginning, "thirst" has been insistent throughout the whole wide world.

You would have had, first of all, the primitive interpretations of what the longing meant. Then as civilization developed, the thinkers of the Far East and of Greece would have seen their greatest minds go to work on what this thirsty longing signified. Privately, everyone everywhere would raise the question in their own hearts, "What does this yearning mean?" Amidst the many things they did to supplant the longing for water, and what the more sensitive ones used for momentary relief from the aching longing that nothing seemed to fill, the question remained.

In different civilizations at different times mass "Thirstian" movements arose, offering theories to help fill this need. Naturally there were rival claims as to which did so the best, and there were even wars waged against one another as a means of asserting dominance, so convinced were the devotees that theirs was the best and only way.

A school of political and economic thinking arose which convincingly argued this whole "Thirstian" business was used by materialistic capitalists as an opiate to give a quasi-quenching to the masses while they themselves exploited the real world of wealth and power.

As the twin fields of psychology and psychiatry developed, they analyzed the "phenomenon of unquenchable thirst" and the means whereby people had tried to assuage it. There was no doubt about the universal thirst. As recently as the nineteenth century one noted English scientist and naturalist (Darwin) had borne witness to this fact in a worldwide expedition among primitive peoples.

However, about the same time, an Austrian scientist (Freud) gave a possible explanation of this thirst that influenced the view of many. He said that it probably developed in antiquity when our ancestral leaders became deified in the minds of their family and tribal followers as the ones with the ability to quench thirst.

It became fashionable among "Thirstiological" experts to even suggest that leaders like Moses, in the ancient past, had encouraged the notion of thirst, to add authority to their edicts, with the old water-in-the-sky-by-and-by enticement for those who obeyed them.

In recent times there has been a general loss of confidence in the barrage of words. There has even been a rejection of all rational and logical explanation. The prevailing philosophy of life has degenerated into a drink-your-own-thing and if-it-feels-good-drink-it individualism.

Since the one who had created the thirst has in no way explained it nor moved to quench it, how can anyone really know the truth about it? Scientists, religionists, artists, philosophers, psychologists, politicians, sociologists, and economists could propose whatever they liked about the nature of this thirst, even ignore it if it suited their program. Libraries are filled with all that they have had to say. But there is no definitive word of truth. The one who had it, held it close, and denied the benefit of it to those who needed it most.

I want to make the bold proposition that if there is such a God, he is a bad God. He is responsible by default for the whole blooming mess in which we find ourselves and the world. The blame for the personal anguish and corporate social chaos we lay at his feet. Anyone who would create a humanity with all the longing and searching that history has revealed is ours, and never have given one solitary firm and certain revelation, is a wicked God.

He has indeed created humanity with an unquenchable spiritual thirst, but never supplied the water to drink. At the personal level we go through life longing with parched mouths for something to drink, not understanding exactly what, and not able to come to terms with what ails us spiritually.

At a societal level, all the potential we had to build a wonderful world got warped and misexpressed and came out awfully wrong. This God cannot hold us accountable or level any blame. We didn't know any better how to build. He had not told us. It followed we had to be confused about sexuality, family, society, and the use of wealth and power. It has been trial and error all the way. We muddle along century by century, exploiting and being exploited, and it is all his fault.

There are several other conclusions we would be forced to admit concerning this anonymous God.

God Is a Tormentor

Not only would our anonymous God be wicked, he would be positively tormenting. For when he saw how things went wrong, he did not move to offer any remedy. In the midst of the human excesses of the powerful and the personal anguish of the weak, he whispers not a divine word. He just watches. If your thinking process works anything like mine you are probably tempted to leap forward to the question, "What if God has spoken as you Christians say; isn't the world still messed up all the same?" But I want you to persist with the question at hand. The average contemporary man (or woman), "has been accustomed, ever since he was a boy, to having half a dozen incompatible philosophies dancing about together in his head."[1] What is more, we never get one of them resolved because we toss thoughts back and forth within our heads like the proverbial hot potato. I want us to settle once and for all that an unrevealing, noncommunicative God is wicked as we understand wickedness.

Should Not Be Sought or Worshiped

It follows that we will have to leave behind the fondly held opinion that this God should be sought after and worshiped. We will have to reject the very idea that all the world's religions are doing what is right and proper in their quest to understand this God and in their encouragement of others to pursue him. Better that they flee such a God.

The truth is that in the spirit of our age we have wanted to avoid a judgmental discriminating spirit. Let me again quote C. S. Lewis in the preface to his book The Great Divorce:

Blake wrote the Marriage of Heaven and Hell. If I have written of their Divorce, this is not because I think myself a fit
antagonist for so great a genius, nor even because I feel at
all sure that I know what he meant. But in some sense or
other the attempt to make that marriage is perennial. The
attempt is based on the belief that reality never presents
us with an absolutely unavoidable "either-or"; that, granted
skill and patience and (above all) time enough, some way
of embracing both alternatives can always be found; that
mere development or adjustment or refinement will somehow turn evil into good without our being called on for a
final and total rejection of anything we should like to retain. This belief I take to be a disastrous error. You cannot
take all luggage with you on all journeys. . . . We are not living in a world where all roads are radii of a circle and
where all, if followed long enough, will therefore draw
gradually nearer and finally meet at the centre; rather [we
live] in a world where every road, after a few miles, forks
into two again, and at each fork you must make a decision.
Even on the biological level life is not like a pool but like
a tree. It does not move towards unity but away from it
and the creatures grow further apart as they increase in
perfection.[2]

He Is Too Small

"Your God is too small," wrote J. B. Phillips, author of
the most excellent New Testament in Modern English. Too
small, not vast, describes a God who was not able to communicate the truth about himself to his world.

Further, while it sounds grand to say that all religions
have aspects of the truth but none has been given "the
truth" because "the truth," like God, is too vast for any one
of them to receive it, we miss the point that most agnostics talk about an anonymous God who has not directly
communicated any truth at all. We are not even talking
about a confusing God who has sprinkled little bits of truth
here and there among the religions of the world for us to

discover like jewels scattered in an Everest of refuse. It will not do to mask the ambiguity of it all by describing this God as vast.

In a world that worships intellect, one of the reasons that so many have chosen to reject the Judeo/Christian revelation of God is that it seems so restricting. So we have such works as Religion Without Revelation first published by Julian Huxley in 1929 and then a later work of his, Evolutionary Ethics, 1943, which devises a system of society and morality without an authoritative foundation. One scholar critiques another and as one theory passes on to the bookshelves, another comes off the press.

At first blush it looks so intellectually stimulating, and some would even say honest, to lay aside preconceived limitations. But in the name of intellectual freedom we have seen the world of rationality and reason reduced to absurdity. In the place of divine revelation we have raised up human chaos. Instead of the ad gloriam of God we have the ad nauseam of man.

There is no doubt that the agnostic proposition of "no revealed truth from on high" has looked like freedom. James A. Froude, the nineteenth century historian, in his biography of Thomas Carlyle, writes, "The agnostic doctrines, he [Carlyle] once said to me, were to appearance like finest flour, from which you might expect the most excellent bread; but when you come to feed on it, you found it was powdered glass, and you had been eating the deadliest poison."[3]

I would advocate the need for intellectual inquiry to be joined to the concept of revealed truth. There is a sense in which a kite is restricted by the line that holds it against the wind. But it is only free to be all that a kite can be while it is held by that line. Sever the line and the kite falls limply to the ground. What looked like freedom denied the kite its very kiteness.

The God Who Is There and Has Spoken

Now, let us tell about the God who has chosen to reveal himself. Before we proceed, I want to make a recommendation. From here on, each time you pick up this book to read it I want you to do a very dangerous thing: I want you to pray. The prayer is for "an agnostic." Read it through and see if it expresses in an honest way what you feel. If not, alter as necessary for yourself.

The Agnostic's Prayer

Living Lord God, I am not sure if you are really there or if I am talking to myself. If you are there, I begin by acknowledging that there are all kinds of obstacles to my coming to you in real faith. I am not even sure if I want you to remove them, because I don't want to get too close to you; I don't want to change certain things about my life. If you are there, Lord, I realize there is a whole new world waiting for me which is rather frightening. Give me the personal courage to ask you to reveal yourself to me. As I read on in this book, show me the truth. And if you are there and care about me and want me to know you, bring me into a genuine relationship with yourself.

Help me not to turn back but keep on until I am where you want me. If you are for real, Lord, and there is the possibility of joyful confidence in this life, and the assurance of heaven as my home, I don't want to miss either. So here I am, Lord, making myself as available to you as I dare at this moment. If you are there, thank you for hearing me. Amen.

This third option, that there really is a God and he has spoken, is the one to which I would lead you. In discussing the first two options, "There is no God" and "There is a God who has not revealed himself," I set forth some logical real-life applications for you to consider, hoping they would lead you to reject those options for what they are—totally unacceptable and unreasonable representations of reality.

In a sense I have not enjoyed this exercise. As Francis Schaeffer says,

> There is no romanticism as one seeks to move a man in the direction of honesty. On the basis of his system you are pushing him further and further towards that which is not only totally against God, but also against himself. You are pushing him out of the real universe, and of course it hurts, of course it is dark in the place where a man, in order to be consistent to his non-Christian presuppositions, must deny what is there in this life as well as in the next.[4]

There are some prerequisites we must understand before we seek the God who has chosen to reveal himself.

First, when we speak of God revealing himself we are automatically making the assumption that God is self-aware. He knows who he is. He understands who he is. He is a self-conscious entity with individual intelligence. That is, he has a mind of his own. He is not a figment of our imagination. He is not dependent on our believing he is there in order to have an existence. Rather, we were created by him as a product of his imagination, and our existence is dependent upon him.

So when God speaks, he speaks from his own self-conscious awareness. And just as we in our self-consciousness are aware of others and can choose to relate to them and reveal our innermost selves to them, so God in his self-consciousness is aware of us, and shows himself to us that we might know him intimately and personally.

This chosen self-expression is imperative to the knowledge of any personage. Unless we choose to reveal ourselves, others will never know who we are. They may try to interpret what we are like from observation, but that is fraught with all the limitations of misjudgment. We know from our experience of family life how easy it is to misread another's intentions. After years of marriage, tremendous efforts still have to be made by husband and wife to communicate, otherwise distortions quickly take over.

So no matter how close and dependent our common everyday relationships may be, we still have the necessity of self-explanation and self-disclosure. How much more so must this be the case if we are to know God. When the Bible asks the question, "Canst thou by searching find out God?" (Job 11:7 KJV), the implied answer is, "Of course not." Just as we cannot know each other without self-disclosure, we cannot know God unless he reveals himself to us.

Second, God wants to relate. When we speak of God acting in self-revelation, there are several other things which we take to be self-evident. For instance, it is only reasonable to assume that if God has communicated to us he really wanted to. We are not talking of a begrudged self-revelation. We are not proposing a God who plays cosmic hide-and-seek, dropping little clues here and there which we must separate from the superfluous or the erroneous. In other words, God is not a transcendent Agatha Christie, and we mere mortal detectives trying to sift out his plot and interpret his clues until, at last, because we are clever enough we understand what is the real story.

If God were like this, how would we ever distinguish between the true and the false? Granted the problem of interpretation remains, but I want us to avoid falling again into the trap of suggesting that God, by the way he has chosen to hide rather than show himself, is directly responsible for the inevitable chaos that would follow.

We acknowledge once again that there are many reasons we may not be open to God's sharing himself with us, just as we have already discussed. Consequently we may be closed to what he is saying, or we may even deliberately try to misrepresent it. When one party is mute or blinkered to another's advances, communication is extremely hindered. Despite this limitation, let us not lose sight of our proposition that God fully intends to relate himself to us as one person to another, so that we can know him and enter into a personal relationship with him.

Third, God is a person. Having said so much we have to acknowledge that there is a way of thinking about God which denies that he is a self-conscious being. Rather, the Divine is understood to be the sum total of all that is. "Pantheists usually believe that God . . . animates the universe as you animate your body: that the universe almost is God, so that if it did not exist He would not exist either, and anything you find in the universe is a part of God."[5] Inherently this God does not have individual personhood. He is sometimes referred to as a "blind life force" with no distinct self that can enter into personal relationships.

We reject this notion of God in its own terms and because of its own premises. For we know that there was a time when this planet had no people on it. At that time, according to our theory under review, the Divine was "all that there was"—and it did not include personhood, for there were no people. It is our contention that the impersonal can never be an adequate cause or explanation for the personal, and therefore can never give rise to personhood.

It is at this selfsame point that we reject atheistic science, anthropology, and philosophy. It is not just "life" we are talking about but personhood.

> The two alternatives are very clear cut. Either there is a personal beginning to everything or one has what the impersonal throws up by chance out of the time sequence. The fact that the second alternative may be veiled by connotation words makes no difference. The words used by Eastern Pantheism; the new theological words such as "Tillich's ground of being"; the secular shift from mass to energy or motion, all eventually come back to the impersonal, plus time, plus chance. If this is really the only answer to man's personality then personality is no more than an illusion, a

kind of sick joke which no amount of semantic juggling will alter. Only some form of mystical jump will allow us to accept that personality comes from impersonality. This was the position into which Teilhard de Chardin was forced. His answer is only a mystical answer to words.

Because these men will not accept the only explanation which can fit the facts of their own experience, they have become metaphysical magicians. No one has presented an idea, let alone demonstrated it to be feasible, to explain how the impersonal beginning plus time plus chance, can give personality. We are distracted by a flourish of endless words, and lo, personality has appeared out of the hat![6]

The god to which these people refer cannot speak. This god has not spoken. This god is indeed dead.

The God Who Has Spoken

With these considerations in mind we move on to consider the God who is there and has spoken. He is able to do so because he is a self-conscious God who knows himself and wants us to know him too. The primary reason for believing in this God is not simply to meet a philosophical necessity which we have postured, but because this God has indeed made himself known.

I am going to present the evidence that shows why Christians believe God has spoken clearly. There is tremendous confusion in the minds of most people concerning God, because they are looking for proof. You often hear people say, "Prove it to me." But there is no such thing as proof for anything unless we are willing to accept the evidence for it. What makes a thing a "proof" to you is evidence you trust or believe in. It is in this sense that we all live by faith every day of our lives, placing faith in the evidences we first perceive and then trust.

For instance, I remember speaking to a student at the Chautauqua Institute in New York. As we talked about different kinds of evidence I asked her, "Do you believe the huge trees which stand across the street are really there?" She said, "No!" Her reason for such an unexpected answer was that she had been on all kinds of hallucinogenic drugs and had seen all kinds of things which were not there. Consequently, she no longer trusted the evidence of her sight. She suffered from flashbacks, and for her, seeing was not believing. The evidence of her eyesight was no longer a proof to her. She therefore did not believe in it.

You have a similar circumstance with people who have suffered from paranoid schizophrenia. One of the marks of this illness is the hearing of voices which are not there. I remember a school teacher who came to see me who subsequently was diagnosed as a paranoid schizophrenic. She heard other teachers talking about her at school and her problems described to the whole school over the P.A. system. She even said the news commentator on TV had mentioned her by name.

The road to recovery is very difficult, as you can imagine. There is often the haunting doubt that what is heard may not be real. The evidence of hearing is no longer the proof it used to be. What Christians believe then is the evidence that God has taken action in history and made himself known.

It is at this point we state emphatically that Christian faith is not a blind existential leap into the dark, but a step into the light of reasonable evidence.

I am aware that this is a remarkable claim. But the reasons for it are no less remarkable. Perhaps what is most remarkable in this age of exalted learning is that so few have ever seriously considered the evidence or heard an intelligent presentation.

The primary evidence that God has spoken is Jesus Christ. He is not just a verbal communication but a living communication. The Christian contends that God has not just spoken an audible word but has come as the living

Word. "And the Word became flesh and dwelt among us, full of grace and truth; we have beheld his glory, glory as of the only Son from the Father" (John 1:14). "He reflects the glory of God and bears the very stamp of his nature, upholding the universe by his word of power" (Heb. 1:3).

There are three areas of study which make it difficult to draw any other conclusion. The following chapters set forth an explanation of these three sets of "evidence."

1. The words of Christ endorsed by the life of Christ
2. The Old Testament prophecy about the Messiah, fulfilled in Jesus Christ
3. The evidence of the resurrection of Jesus Christ.

For Reflection and Discussion

1. Can you think of another fundamental option than:
   a. there is no God
   b. there is a God who has chosen not to reveal himself
   c. there is a God who has chosen to reveal himself?
2. Do you think it takes more faith to believe there is no God than to believe there is a God?
3. Can you think of another reason to do what we normally think of as "right" than the pragmatic one that "it seems to work best"?
4. Do you agree that the anonymous God who deliberately remains silent concerning himself and his designs for the world is a bad God?
5. Given the fact that the world has gone sadly awry, what is the fundamental difference between a God who has not spoken and a God who has?
6. In what other ways can an anonymous God be said to be wicked and unattractive?

7. Discuss the difference between the two concepts:
   a. an unselfconscious impersonal God
   b. a personal God who knows himself and can relate to us.

   For instance:
   a. Could you have a personal relationship with a God who was the sum total of everything?
   b. Could an impersonal God hold you accountable for sin or extend forgiveness?

8. From your own experience in the world of business and family life, discuss the relationship between evidence and proof.

9. Did the Agnostic's Prayer help?

5

The Words and Life of Jesus

⬭ir Winston Churchill said there are three things that can be asked of any statement to determine its real content and worth: What was said? How was it said? and Who said it? He then went on to draw the conclusion that the most important of these is the last, Who said it?

From the time of Jesus' life on earth, and all the way up to this present moment, one question has inevitably arisen when people discuss him. It is, Who is he? The way we answer that question will determine in what measure we value the teaching of Jesus. An avenue of investigation that is rarely pursued in this search is one in which the quality of his life and the content of his teaching are viewed alongside each other. The object of this section is to set words of Jesus in the light of the life of Jesus so that we can help determine the identity of Jesus.

One thing we are obliged to acknowledge is that Jesus Christ made extraordinary claims for himself. What makes those claims all the more extraordinary is not the audacity which is implied, but the extraordinary quality of life that was lived out by the man who uttered them. For while his claims are of a megalomaniac order he in no way comes across as megalomaniac.

We read of Alexander the Great weeping because he had no more worlds to conquer. We know that Napoleon Bonaparte set the crown on his own head at his coronation. He alone was worthy and he alone was the center of the ritual. We remember the raging antics of Adolf Hitler, who desired not only to rule the world, but create a super race that would rule forever. We suspect the egos of all who aspire to leadership.

But when Jesus speaks he does not come across as a fanatic or a self-centered prima donna, much less a madman or an egomaniac. While others in history have exercised their greatness and power by demanding obeisance, Jesus Christ led in the garb and spirit of a servant. Whether among the poor, the derelict and deprived, the rich and fortunate, or those who used their power corruptly out of cowardice, Jesus is the one who knows who he is and speaks with firm confidence. He comes across as an integrated and whole person, not serving out of weakness but out of strength; not under, but in control.

This is the reason the skeptics, and even enemies of Christianity, are ready to declare that Jesus was a great teacher. You often hear it said that he was even a prophet. The amazing thing is that he claimed to be neither. But he did claim to be God, not in the sense that Heinlein in his book Stranger in a Strange Land claimed all men to be God, "I am God, you are God, we are God," the same sense in which those of the Pantheistic religions claim to be God. For Jesus, as a Jew, understood that God was not a part of everything, but was apart from everything. The God of the Jew was the one who made it all, ex nihilo, out of nothing.

But how often you hear people say that he never claimed to be God! Those who say such have never read the record in the Gospels of what Jesus actually said. Here are some of his extraordinary claims:

The Source of Life

"I am the true vine, and my Father is the vinedresser. Every branch of mine that bears no fruit, he takes away, and every branch that does bear fruit he prunes, that it may bear more fruit. You are already made clean by the word which I have spoken to you. Abide in me, and I in you. As the branch cannot bear fruit by itself, unless it abides in the vine, neither can you, unless you abide in me. I am the vine, you are the branches. He who abides in me, and I in him, he it is that bears much fruit, for apart from me you can do nothing. If a man does not abide in me, he is cast forth as a branch and withers; and the branches are gathered, thrown into the fire and burned. If you abide in me, and my words abide in you, ask whatever you will, and it shall be done for you. By this my Father is glorified, that you bear much fruit, and so prove to be my disciples" (John 15:1–8).

We have become so well acquainted with words like these we miss what is being said. Would you not expect Jesus to say that the Father is the true vine and he, Jesus, the one who tends to the pruning? But no, Jesus claims to be the true vine, that is, the true source of life, and declares his Father to be the pruner.

Further, Jesus says in this context that if we are joined to him, the vine, we shall be productive, and if not, we shall wither and die, and like dead wood be cast into the fire to be burned. The direct implication is that a person's earthly usefulness and his eternal well-being are both dependent on his being grafted into Christ. Christ is obviously asserting divine prerogatives for himself, and not in the same sense as those who think we are all part of the divine. He is not claiming to be a piece of the divine in the form of man but the source of the divine for all humankind.

Divine Forgiveness

"But that you may know that the Son of man has authority on earth to forgive sins," he said (Luke 5:24). "Your sins are forgiven you" (Luke 5:20).

We can easily grasp how a man forgives offenses against himself. Someone deliberately misrepresents your motives and you forgive them. But Jesus claims to forgive other people their sins, not against himself, but against God. The religious leaders who heard these words said, "Who can forgive sins but God" and accused Jesus of blasphemy. They fully understood the divine action that Jesus presumed to adopt as his own right. Jesus in turn made no apology for it, nor did he seek to weaken the impact of what he said.

If anything, he strengthened the force of what he claimed. "But that you may know that the Son of man has authority on earth to forgive sins . . ." (Luke 5:24).

Power over Death

"I am the resurrection and the life; he who believes in me, though he die, yet shall he live, and whoever lives and believes in me shall never die" (John 11:25, 26).

Now Jesus has moved from the blasphemous—if he be not God—forgiving sins to the ridiculous granting of eternal life. These words in John 11 always sound comforting and reassuring when read at a funeral. There is something appropriately solemn and yet beautiful about them. But they were taken on the lips of Jesus not as a man speaks poetry but as an authoritative statement about death.

While the lost and despairing philosophers of our civilization can only agree that death is the one ultimate truth that is absolutely true for all of us, Jesus says that to believe in him is to overcome death, and to live forever.

Christ's Preexistence

"Before Abraham was, I am" (John 8:58). Read the full account of this in your Bible. There are two claims Jesus is making, both of which drove the religious leaders of his day to try and do away with him. The first was that he existed before Abraham and that he was, thereby, "greater than" he. Abraham was the revered father of Judaism, and had been dead some two thousand years, give or take a couple of centuries.

But even more stunning to the Jews was the phrase "I AM." This is the name by which God made himself known to Moses. "I AM WHO I AM" (Exod. 3:14). And Moses was to tell the enslaved children of Israel that "I AM" had sent him (Exod. 3:14). You can see from the response of the Jews to Jesus in his day that they understood his claim. They sought to destroy him. In no way did they think that he was a great teacher.

Jesus a King

"My kingship is not of this world" (John 18:36), said Jesus to Pilate as he stood on trial for his life. The cunning accusation had been made that Jesus claimed to be a king. Within the Roman empire, Caesar was king. Any challenge to that sovereignty was automatically met with death. "Are you a king?" asked the Roman governor. To which Jesus gave the answer, "My kingship is not of this world." But what is Jesus acknowledging? That he is a king, because he does have a kingdom. In contempt Pilate put in three languages of the day the title, "King of the Jews" over the cross of Jesus. And even then, those who had plotted his death could not leave it alone. "Say that he said he was," they asked of Pilate. "Change the wording!" But it was left to stand.

Christ's Identity with the Father

"I and the Father are one" (John 10:30). With this statement, we move from implied divinity to explicit claim.

In the case of this quotation it is clear from the response of the Jews that Jesus was understood to be claiming divinity: "The Jews answered him, 'We stone you for no good work but for blasphemy; because you, being a man, make yourself God'" (John 10:33).

Jesus was not simply asserting oneness of purpose with the Father, but oneness of nature. It follows logically then, that to meet Jesus is to meet the Father. "He who has seen me has seen the Father." Read carefully the context of this statement: Philip, one of the disciples, has asked Jesus to show them the Father (John 14:9). Jesus asked, "Have I been with you so long, and yet you do not know me, Philip? He who has seen me has seen the Father; how can you say, 'Show us the Father'?"

While this statement raises questions as to the exact meaning of his identity with his Father in heaven (a question, by the way, which was thrashed out for the first four centuries of Christian history), there is absolutely no doubt that Jesus was claiming, in unmistakable terms, such an identity with the Father as made him, Jesus, a participant in the divine nature of God himself.

Now these are but a smattering of the extraordinary things that Jesus said of himself. If he were merely a man, "great teacher" would be the last thing we should call him.

C. S. Lewis sums up the issue this way.

I am trying here to prevent anyone saying the really foolish thing that people often say about Him: "I'm ready to accept Jesus as a great moral teacher, but I don't accept His claim to be God." That is the one thing we must not say. A man who was merely a man and said the sort of things Jesus said would not be a great moral teacher. He would be either a lunatic—on a level with the man who says he is a poached egg—or else he would be the Devil of Hell. You must make your choice. Either this man was, and is, the Son of God: or else a madman or something worse. You can shut Him up for a fool, you can spit at Him and kill Him as a demon, or you can fall at His feet and call Him Lord and God. But let us not come with any patronising nonsense about His being a great human teacher. He has not left that open to us. He did not intend to.[1]

For Reflection and Discussion

1. Which evidence for Christ's divinity did you find the most convincing?
    a. Jesus as the source of life
    b. Jesus exercising divine forgiveness
    c. Jesus claiming power over death
    d. the preexistence of Christ
    e. Jesus' claim to sovereignty
    f. Jesus' claim to oneness with the Father
2. From your knowledge of the Gospels, what other sayings of Jesus are equally remarkable?
3. If Christ is really God in the flesh, should Christians low-key it, and even pretend otherwise so as not to be offensive to those who disagree?
4. Are we more sensitive to the feelings of people than we are to the feelings of God?

6

Old Testament Prophecy

rophecy is a unique kind of evidence to show the reality of God, even though it is dangerous to claim. Most of us are aware of the manipulation of historical events and prophetic forecasts so that they appear to match one another. We are also aware of the notoriety of eccentric groups which catch the headlines. Nearly every other year in recent times there is the prediction that the world is going to end on a given day and at a particular time. The media is fascinated with the spectacular commitment of people selling all they own and waiting in the mountains or some such place for the return of Christ. We read it with interest, wonder if the latest sect is right, but pay it very little attention.

More than likely you have entered into discussion with Mormons or Jehovah's Witnesses. Certainly they have knocked at your door. Possibly you have purchased their literature. You may have watched Garner Ted Armstrong on television or seen his magazine Plain Truth. All these sects make much of prophecy. International events are cited as fulfillment of prophecy. Large tracts of history are shown to fit predictions of either the Bible or their leaders. To say the very least we are skeptical.

The reason prophecy is so important is that it indicates supernatural intervention in history. That is why the sects go to such pains to align prophetic utterance with the events of the times, to give supernatural authority to their teaching.

Despite the dangers and excesses which are cause for skepticism we cannot escape the claims that Jesus came as the fulfillment of centuries-old prophecy. For a start he said as much about himself. "'The Spirit of the Lord is upon me, because he has anointed me to preach good news to the poor. He has sent me to proclaim release to the captives and recovering of sight to the blind, to set at liberty those who are oppressed, to proclaim the acceptable year of the Lord.' And he closed the book, and gave it back to the attendant, and sat down; and the eyes of all in the synagogue were fixed on him. And he began to say to them, 'Today this scripture has been fulfilled in your hearing'" (Luke 4:18–21).

Prophecy is one of the evidences that demonstrates God's supernatural intervention into the world in the person of Christ. When considered alongside the other evidences which point to the historical uniqueness of Jesus, prophecy finds its proper place and must come under our scrutiny.

Further, we need to understand the full implication of completed prophecy. We have already mentioned the authority that it lends to any who can make its claims good, and Christians no less grasp the significance to their cause.

But what we are discussing is the evidence that there is a God who has revealed himself. If prophecy can be shown to be true, apart from anything God may be directly telling us in the prophecy, it also tells us that there really is a God and he is at pains to make himself known. Prophecy also tells us something about the amazing foreknowledge of God. He knows the happenings of history before they take place. That is, he is outside time and not limited in his knowledge by the restriction of events in linear sequence.

Additionally, God has the power to bring about events as he predicts. History then is not outside God's influence nor is he a helpless bystander. He is at work in the ebb and flow of international politics. Yes, we make our choices and live with their consequences, but God is also working out his own personal designs as well.

History then is not a meaningless jumble of events that carries us all off into obscurity. Rather, it moves toward a destination in which God is ultimately going to triumph.

This automatically raises questions: Why then is the history of civilization littered with so many monuments to misery? If there really is a God why did he not make things work out differently?

While there are no easy answers, we can understand that part of what it means to be human is having a will with which to choose. It also follows that God, if he wanted us to love, whether it be himself or one another, had to allow the possibility that we could choose otherwise. Without the power to choose we would disembowel the very notion of love. If God had automated a response called love from us toward himself or others, then it would not have been love as we understand it, a love which springs from a free response. We find the concept of a "puppet on a string" love as repulsive as the automatons produced by genetic engineering in Aldous Huxley's Brave New World.

The tension we find impossible to resolve is between men and women who make history what it is by the actions they choose, and an all-powerful God, who is in the midst of the chaos we have created, working out his own divine purpose; and not only so, but being able to forecast certain events and then orchestrate them even as nations continue to "do their own thing."

But the more amazing thing, as we shall see, is that God foretold of his direct entrance into the human scene, and then joined himself to our human plight. More than that, it was the ordained role of the Messiah not only to suffer with us but to suffer for us.

So we come to the Bible prophecies to which I would draw your attention. They pertain to Jesus the Christ, that is, the Messiah. The title Christ is the Greek form of the Hebrew word Messiah, and since the New Testament was written in Greek, the international language of the first century, it is the title by which we normally ascribe Messiahship to Jesus.

More specifically, we are going to deal with the prophecies concerning his birth and his death. When the Bible speaks about these it always has a dual focus; (1) the identity of Jesus, who he is; and (2) the mission of Jesus, what he came to do. These are inseparable in their significance. Who Jesus is makes possible what he came to do.

A second set of relationships is between the events prophesied and what they mean. In other words, God was not initiating prophecy in order to perform magic and thereby convince people of his existence and power. The claim of the prophets is that God was going to act in history to achieve certain objectives which were both important to humanity's well-being and essential to his design for individual human destinies. We will therefore investigate not just the events prophesied, but the prophets' explanation of what God is going to do.

My use of Bible prophecy will be within the flow of Christian tradition as always understood by orthodox Christians over the centuries. If you are even vaguely familiar with the Christian faith you will see this immediately.

Prophecy Concerning the Birth of Jesus

"But you, O Bethlehem Ephrathah, who are little to be among the clans of Judah, from you shall come forth for me one who is to be ruler in Israel, whose origin is from of old, from ancient days. Therefore he shall give them up until the time when she who is in travail has brought forth; then the rest of his brethren shall return to the people of Israel. And he shall stand and feed his flock in the strength of the LORD, in the majesty of the name of the LORD his God. And they shall dwell secure, for now he shall be great to the ends of the earth" (Mic. 5:2–4).

Micah gives to us three distinctive prophetic words concerning the Messiah:

1. His birthplace
2. His sovereignty
3. His ancient origin

His Birthplace

Jesus was born in Bethlehem. But that is not where his parents lived. Their home was in Nazareth. It was the circumstance of a Roman census ordered by Caesar Augustus that brought Joseph and Mary to Bethlehem. Rome had determined to make the count in some measure according to the Jewish understanding of themselves, by descendency. No less an authority than Sir W. M. Ramsay maintains that Quirinius (Luke 2:2) was not only governor of Syria, but that he controlled Syria's foreign relations and supervised the census.

In any case, all the house of David went to be enrolled in Bethlehem, which was the family seat. This was a journey of over eighty miles by foot, not an inconsiderable hardship for a woman whose pregnancy was close to full term. It may have been softened some by the prospect of passing through Jerusalem, which was on their way, since just the sight of Jerusalem was the joy of every Jewish pilgrim.

In the midst of all these real-life circumstances, a prophecy given centuries before was entering into the pages of history. The mighty wheels of Roman power politics were turning to make Bethlehem a maternity ward for the promised Messiah.

It may have crossed your mind to ask, "Was this prophecy of Micah really intended to describe the Messiah?" Fortunately, we are not left to answer that question in the isolation of the twentieth century.

It needs to be recognized that the Messiah was no new subject of study for the Jew living in enemy occupied Palestine under the heel of Roman domination. The hope of a Messiah, a deliverer, was in their hearts and on their lips. An air of expectancy was surging in the life stream of the Jewish people.

So when the wise men came into Jerusalem, looking for one "born king of the Jews," Herod assembled "all the chief priests and scribes of the people" and "inquired of them where the Christ [Messiah] was to be born" (see Matt. 2:2–4).

Their response appears to have been immediate, as if already there was a general consensus among them—a remarkable thing for Jewish rabbis—or any group of religious leaders for that matter. They told him, "In Bethlehem of Judea; for so it is written by the prophet"! They then proceeded to quote Micah 5:2, the prophecy at which we have been looking. The findings of the Jewish theologians were passed on by Herod to the magi who then went on their way to Bethlehem to find the baby Jesus, the Messiah.

But our question has been answered. Even though Jewish leaders were to become violent opponents of Jesus when he entered into public prominence some thirty years later, at the time of his birth those whom King Herod summoned as "expert witnesses" understood Micah 5:2 to be a messianic prophecy.

The Messiah's Sovereignty

The reference to Matthew 2 and the search of the magi from the East bring us to the designation ruler. Remember the Eastern seers were looking for a newborn "king." On the strength of expert advice they were sent to Bethlehem. Herod, then king, felt threatened by the implications that somewhere out there his replacement was waiting in the wings. At the very least it meant that the heir was not to be from his family line. Worse still, it augured his own demise.

Under the guise of also wanting to pay homage to this King he told the foreign envoys to report back when they had found him. His intentions, however, were to eliminate the supplanter, which later led to the slaughter of some estimated twenty to thirty baby boys in the Bethlehem area.

The claim of sovereignty was clearly associated with the office of the Messiah. This is further endorsed by the words of Isaiah: "Of the increase of his government and of peace there will be no end, upon the throne of David, and over his kingdom, to establish it, and to uphold it with justice and with righteousness from this time forth and for evermore. The zeal of the LORD of hosts will do this" (Isa. 9:7).

We saw in the previous chapter that it was the accusation that he claimed to be a king that brought Jesus to trial before the Roman authorities. As ludicrous as the sight was of Jesus gibbeted to the cross with the title "King of the Jews" pinned over his head, he died as he had been born, not only in demeaning circumstances but also as King.

In human terms there was very little that could be called kingly about Jesus. This fact is epitomized in what has been designated his triumphal entry into Jerusalem (Luke 19:28–38). He rode into Jerusalem not on a horse but on a colt, the foal of an ass. There were only a few garments thrown across the colt; no fine saddle riding high. It was not the city people who acclaimed him but the peasant folk who were also making their way into Jerusalem for the Passover.

But their cries, "Blessed is the King who comes in the name of the Lord" (Luke 19:38), symbolized three things:

First, the messianic figure of the one who would sit on the throne of David was moving irrevocably toward that destiny.

Second, the messianic age of the kingdom of God was about to begin as King Jesus entered into his kingdom.

Third, his kingdom was "not of this world" not only because it was spiritual but because it emphasized humility and servanthood as against pride and lordly grandeur.

> Ride on, ride on in majesty!
> In lowly pomp ride on to die:
> O Christ, Thy triumphs now begin
> O'er captive death and conquered sin.

> Ride on, ride on in majesty!
> In lowly pomp ride on to die;
> Bow Thy meek head to mortal pain,
> Then take, O God, thy power, and reign.

> Henry H. Milman, 1827

The Messiah's Preexistence

With the prophecy of the Messiah's preexistence we move into what has been termed "the mystery of the incarnation." The word incarnation literally means "in the flesh." The overwhelming evidence of the prophets is that the Messiah would be God Incarnate—God clothed in humanity.

Micah 5:2 puts it this way, ". . . whose origin is from of old, from ancient days." Isaiah's word concerning the Messiah is much better known due to Handel: "For to us a child is born, to us a son is given; and the government will be upon his shoulder, and his name will be called 'Wonderful Counselor, Mighty God, Everlasting Father, Prince of Peace'" (Isa. 9:6).

It is hard to read this without hearing in one's head the cadence of Handel's Messiah with full orchestra. The remarkable claim for the coming Messiah's preexistence is summed up in the title "Everlasting Father." It literally means "Father from all times."

Take note, however, that Isaiah has already designated this child yet to be born as "Mighty God." When this thought is joined to Isaiah's earlier words, "Behold, a young woman shall conceive and bear a son, and shall call his name Immanuel" (Isa. 7:14), you are left with no other conclusion than that the Messiah was to be God himself—for the name Immanuel means "God with us."

The New Testament writers understood this clearly: "Now the birth of Jesus Christ took place in this way. When his mother Mary had been betrothed to Joseph, before they came together she was found to be with child of the Holy Spirit; . . . 'Behold, a virgin shall conceive and bear a son, and his name shall be called Emmanuel' (which means, God with us)" (Matt. 1:18, 23).

"In the beginning was the Word, and the Word was with God, and the Word was God. He was in the beginning with God; all things were made through him, and without him was not anything made that was made. . . . And the Word became flesh and dwelt among us, full of grace and truth; we have beheld his glory, glory as of the only Son from the Father" (John 1:1–3, 14).

"He is the image of the invisible God, the first-born of all creation; for in him all things were created, in heaven and on earth, visible and invisible, whether thrones or dominions or principalities or authorities—all things were created through him and for him. He is before all things, and in him all things hold together" (Col. 1:15–17).

"In many and various ways God spoke of old to our fathers by the prophets; but in these last days he has spoken to us by a Son, whom he appointed the heir of all things, through whom also he created the world. He reflects the glory of God and bears the very stamp of his nature, upholding the universe by his word of power" (Heb. 1:1–3).

Having already reviewed Jesus' claims to divinity, it is only left to me to point out to you that we have been reviewing words of prophecy. These several quotations from the New Testament are only so that you can see how thoroughly those prophecies have come to pass in Jesus Christ, and then how thoroughly they were integrated into the teaching of the first evangelists, the authors of the New Testament.

The prophecies of Micah and Isaiah came from the period 740–700 B.C. They were contemporaries but living in totally different environments. Micah was a rural resident from a little town called Moresheth some thirty miles outside Jerusalem. Isaiah lived in Jerusalem and was familiar with the people and politics of the nation's capital. There is no evidence that they knew each other personally.

The reliability of Isaiah's text bears further note. Among the Dead Sea Scrolls discovered in the 1940s was the text of Isaiah. It is our most ancient copy of the prophet's work. It is dated about the second century B.C. and is virtually identical to the later copies dated in the third and fourth centuries A.D.

Prophecy Concerning the Messiah's Death

There are two prophecies concerning the death of Jesus which we must consider. They are Psalm 22:1, 14–18 and Isaiah 53. Psalm 22 gives details about the crucifixion and Isaiah unfolds its meaning. As we have noted, Isaiah was writing in the second half of the eighth century B.C. Psalm 22 is a psalm of David who lived around 1000 B.C., or nearly three centuries before Isaiah.

The Prophecy of David—Psalm 22

[1]My God, my God, why hast thou forsaken me? Why art thou so far from helping me, from the words of my groaning? [2]O my God, I cry by day, but thou dost not answer; and by night, but find no rest.

[3]Yet thou art holy, enthroned on the praises of Israel. [4]In thee our fathers trusted; they trusted, and thou didst deliver them. [5]To thee they cried, and were saved; in thee they trusted, and were not disappointed.

[6]But I am a worm, and no man; scorned by men, and despised by the people. [7]All who see me mock at me, they

make mouths at me, they wag their heads; [8]He committed his cause to the Lord; let him deliver him, let him rescue him, for he delights in him!"

[9]Yet thou art he who took me from the womb; thou didst keep me safe upon my mother's breasts. [10]Upon thee was I cast from my birth, and since my mother bore me thou hast been my God. [11]Be not far from me, for trouble is near and there is none to help.

[12]Many bulls encompass me, strong bulls of Bashan surround me; [13]they open wide their mouths at me, like a ravening and roaring lion.

[14]I am poured out like water, and all my bones are out of joint; my heart is like wax, it is melted within my breast; [15]my strength is dried up like a potsherd, and my tongue cleaves to my jaws; thou dost lay me in the dust of death.

[16]Yea, dogs are round about me; a company of evildoers encircle me; they have pierced my hands and feet—[17]I can count all my bones—they stare and gloat over me; [18]they divide my garments among them, and for my raiment they cast lots.

[19]But thou, O Lord, be not far off! O thou my help, hasten to my aid! [20]Deliver my soul from the sword, my life from the power of the dog! [21]Save me from the mouth of the lion, my afflicted soul from the horns of the wild oxen!

[22]I will tell of thy name to my brethren; in the midst of the congregation I will praise thee: [23]You who fear the Lord, praise him! all you sons of Jacob, glorify him, and stand in awe of him, all you sons of Israel! [24]For he has not despised or abhorred the affliction of the afflicted; and he has not hid his face from him, but has heard, when he cried to him.

[25]From thee comes my praise in the great congregation; my vows I will pay before those who fear him. [26]The afflicted shall eat and be satisfied; those who seek him shall praise the Lord! May your hearts live forever!

[27]All the ends of the earth shall remember and turn to the Lord; and all the families of the nations shall worship before him. [28]For dominion belongs to the Lord, and he rules over the nations.

[29]Yea, to him shall all the proud of the earth bow down; before him shall bow all who go down to the dust, and he who cannot keep himself alive. [30]Posterity shall serve him; men shall tell of the LORD to the coming generation, [31]and proclaim his deliverance to a people yet unborn, that he has wrought it.

Psalm 22 prophetically sets forth Christ's agonizing emotions on the cross. Verses 14 through 17 are graphic representations of the suffering he endured through crucifixion. There is the "cry of dereliction" from the cross, verse 1 (see Matt. 27:46). And there are the cries of rejection from the crowd, verses 7 and 8 (see Matt. 27:43). There is the physical piercing of the hands and feet, verse 16, and the gambling for the seamless robe of Christ, verse 18 (see Matt. 27:35); the ugliness of a disjointed body that finally collapses, verse 14, which is what happens in crucifixion, causing death by asphyxiation. Even the "counting" of his bones, verse 17, implies that they remained intact. You will remember they broke the bones of the two criminals who were executed with Jesus, but not his. He had already died, and was speared for good measure, just to make sure.

The Prophecy of Isaiah—Isaiah 53:1–12

[1]Who has believed what we have heard? And to whom has the arm of the LORD been revealed? [2]For he grew up before him like a young plant, and like a root out of dry ground; he had no form or comeliness that we should look at him, and no beauty that we should desire him. [3]He was despised and rejected by men; a man of sorrows, and acquainted with grief; and as one from whom men hide their faces he was despised, and we esteemed him not.

[4]Surely he has borne our griefs and carried our sorrows, yet we esteemed him stricken, smitten by God, and afflicted. [5]But he was wounded for our transgressions, he was bruised for our iniquities; upon him was the chastisement that made us whole, and with his stripes we are

healed. [6]All we like sheep have gone astray; we have turned every one to his own way; and the LORD has laid on him the iniquity of us all.

[7]He was oppressed, and he was afflicted, yet he opened not his mouth; like a lamb that is led to the slaughter, and like a sheep that before its shearers is dumb, so he opened not his mouth. [8]By oppression and judgment he was taken away; and as for his generation, who considered that he was cut off out of the land of the living, stricken for the transgression of my people? [9]And they made his grave with the wicked and with a rich man in his death, although he had done no violence, and there was no deceit in his mouth.

[10]Yet it was the will of the LORD to bruise him; he has put him to grief; when he makes himself an offering for sin, he shall see his offspring, he shall prolong his days; the will of the LORD shall prosper in his hand; [11]he shall see the fruit of the travail of his soul and be satisfied; by his knowledge shall the righteous one, my servant, make many to be accounted righteous; and he shall bear their iniquities. [12]Therefore I will divide him a portion with the great, and he shall divide the spoil with the strong; because he poured out his soul to death, and was numbered with the transgressors; yet he bore the sin of many, and made intercession for the transgressors.

Isaiah 53 is the classic Old Testament prophecy on the sufferings of the Messiah. There are details which are strikingly descriptive of Christ's humiliation and death. For instance, his silence before his accusers, verse 7 (see Matt. 26:63; 27:12–14), or dying alongside criminals and then being buried in the grave of the wealthy Joseph of Arimathea, verse 9 (see Matt. 27:57). There is very little doubt that verse 8 indicates judicial murder, which is an exact description of Christ's legal treatment.

Before we move on to the prophesied meaning of these events we stop for a moment to reflect on what we may have just realized for the first time—the extraordinary detail surrounding the prophecies of the trial and execution of Jesus Christ. Even if you put on your most skeptical glasses it is hard to draw any other conclusion than that there really is a supernatural process at work.

For instance, crucifixion was not a known form of execution to either David (1000 B.C.) or Isaiah (740 B.C.). It was the Romans who introduced it as a torturous spectacle meant to act as a deterrent to crime and, more particularly, rebellion.

But supposing, you say, Jesus spotted something in the Old Testament that he could manipulate to his advantage. Suppose he noticed the connection between Psalm 22 (he quoted it on the cross, remember?) and capital punishment. Suppose for a moment he knew he had a good chance of death by crucifixion and thereby could immortalize himself as a messiah—even if it did cost him his life. What do you say about the things over which he had no control? The gambling for his garments, for instance; or the rich Joseph of Arimathea giving him a burial place.

Perhaps one of the most overlooked facts of messianic prophecy as fulfilled by Jesus is that in both his birth and death the Roman government had a direct hand. It was their decreed census that brought Joseph and Mary to Bethlehem, and their condemnation that took him to the cross. If the Jews had done it their way, Jesus would have been stoned for blasphemy.

The point I reiterate is that as mighty as the Roman Empire was in its day, the Lord was working out his own good purpose. Among the decisions of the powerful, the cowardice of the weak, and the machinations of the wicked, and without in any way their behaving other than true to form, God's design to bring mercy and peace, goodness, and enlightenment was being irrevocably fulfilled as spoken by the prophets.

The Meaning of the Messiah's Death

The detail described in the death of the Messiah is remarkable, but even more so is its explicit meaning. Isaiah belabors the point that the suffering borne by the Lord's "servant" (Isa. 53:11) is not on his own account but on behalf of others. The prophet's language comes right from the altar and takes its imagery from the Jewish animal sacrifices.

When the animal was slain, the one seeking forgiveness set his hand on the head of the animal and it was seen to die in his place. The symbolism of the act portrays a life laid down on behalf of another. The animal sacrificed bore away the judgment deserved by the offender. The word used of this act is atonement. It literally means at-one-ment. With the guilt removed the alienated sinner was brought back into relationship (oneness) with God (Lev. 1:4; see again Isaiah 53:4–6). For a full explanation of how Christ fulfilled this, read Hebrews 9 and 10.

The New Testament Understanding of the Messiah's Death

When we look at the New Testament, the prophets' message is spelled out once again. John the Baptist, who was the forerunner of the Messiah, and who understood himself as a fulfillment of prophecy (John 1:23), said of Jesus when he first saw him, "Behold, the Lamb of God, who takes away the sin of the world!" (John 1:29).

Jesus, just before he was snatched into custody, celebrated a last supper with his first followers. At that meal he took a cup of wine and, before he passed it around said, "This is my blood of the covenant, which is poured out for many for the forgiveness of sins" (Matt. 26:28). In that imagery he revealed his own understanding of his death, so soon to take place.

Peter wrote in early A.D. 60, speaking of Jesus, "He himself bore our sins in his body on the tree, that we might die to sin and live to righteousness. By his wounds you have been healed" (1 Peter 2:24).

In these Scriptures concerning the death of Jesus we have come right to the heart of God's self-giving, self-sharing, self-revealing. To me there is a sense of wonder, like a little boy looking into a microscope for the first time and seeing things that he never thought possible.

The Cost of Forgiveness

The cost of forgiveness brings us to the deepness and the darkness of sin. It is no small thing that the everlasting Father, the Prince of Peace, should suffer the grief and humiliation, the darkness and pain of a rebellious, lost world. He assumed all our Godforsakenness, and in a moment of time, bore the alienation and the guilt for all the world for all time. As the evangelist and apostle Paul puts it, He who knew no sin was made sin for us (see 2 Cor. 5:21).

When we ask, "Why should it be this way? Why should God suffer for our sins?" the one thing that begins to filter through the mists of our blindness is the essential and inherent justice which is part of God's very nature.

The answer lies not in a system, but in a person—God. It is because of what God is like. As it is the nature of light to break into a spectrum of color when passed through a crystal, so justice is an inherent part of God's nature, and the way he has therefore made things. You can't ask why. It just is so. As there is the nature of light, so there is the nature of God. When seen in those terms it does not make sense to ask, "Could it be some other way?"

In the deeper moments of our own self-awareness, we know it is much the same with us. When we are aware of another's wrongdoing it hurts us. The wrong may not be directed at us personally but we still feel it. And when that wrong goes unchecked and unjudged there is a profound sense in which we become tainted and wounded with its sickness and share in its guilt.

In our nation at the moment there is a great internal languishing. It is no good our being told that each of us lives to himself or herself, and as long as we don't hurt anyone else we can do as we like. We are all hurt and wounded by the excesses of individualism—"doing your own thing." There is a great pain in the land as we struggle in a society which rejects any objective definition of pornography, for instance. When we go to the courts about it we can't approach the discussion on the basis of what is morally right or wrong, but have to deal with it in terms of arbitrary rules established on no moral basis but on the basis of zoning technicalities. We are all affected by it. We are all stained and made sick by it. It's no good asking the question, "Why should we feel this way?" as if we could make human beings impervious to the impact on them of the society in which they live, and their identification with it, and their responsibility for it.

The real reason is simply that God, being the God he is, when he made us in his image, instilled in us his character traits. No matter how perverted and warped the image has become, we cannot escape our divine origin. When the Bible says we reap what we sow, it is not describing a God with a tally book levying fines against this infringement or that. The Bible is describing the way things are. There is a moral repercussion for every immoral action. There is a "deep justice" and no amount of surface injustice will subvert it.

I recently heard a medical case history discussed on the radio. A man fell into deep despair whenever he heard the news. It became so bad that he could no longer work. He was hospitalized and subjected to a range of therapies until he could hear the awful news of the world and not be thrown into despair. The commentator raised the question as to who was really sick, the one who is wounded and bruised by the incessant stream of bad news with which the media sates us, or the one who is impervious to it? The implicit question was, "Had they cured this man or was he now even more profoundly sick?"

My answer is that he was not cured but cauterized. You are healthy if you hurt when you get burned. You are sick when you don't.

The most moving news in the world is that the Almighty in all his beauty and purity has stepped into our shoes and, out of the power of his love for us, has borne the shame and the guilt of it all. The account of the death of Jesus in the three synoptic Gospels—Matthew, Mark, and Luke—all record that, as he died, a great darkness came over the land (Matt. 27:45; Mark 15:33; and Luke 23:44). Creation itself was overwhelmed by the darkness of the moment of judgment that Christ embraced for the whole world. But by the miracle of what the Bible calls "grace," "He was wounded for our transgressions, he was bruised for our iniquities . . . and with his stripes we are healed" (Isa. 53:5).

Conclusion of Comments on Prophecy

As we close this section on the evidence that messianic prophecy presents to us, there are several further observations that should not be missed. The prophets, as they foretold of the Messiah, made known truths which could hardly have sprung from their own religion. For in a very distinctive way they spoke of things which were vastly outside the realm of their own religious experience, indeed appeared to be against the religion they had inherited from their forefathers. Yet because many of us are familiar with those prophecies as fulfilled in Christ, we tend to overlook the uniqueness of the message the prophets gave to us.

The Taking of Human Form

One of the reasons that Jesus was rejected as the Messiah was that he came as a man. It was alien to any Jewish conception of God that God should be tainted and defiled by humanity. They had indeed learned well of the holiness of God and the utter separation that must exist between God and sinful humankind. So when Jesus spent time with the immoral and social outcasts, it just heightened the Jewish antagonism to the whole implied blasphemy.

There is no way that Isaiah or Micah could have dreamed up the incarnation from their own religious experience and imagination.

Human Sacrifice

In a Jewish context it is no less astounding that the Messiah was to die on behalf of sinful humankind. Human sacrifice was a pagan practice. It was anathema to the Jew.

We have become too well acquainted with the Good Friday drama, and need to see with refreshed vision what God had foretold was to happen. Jesus, a man, would die for all men.

World Focus

The Messiah was not simply to be a deliverer for the Jewish people but for the world. He was to be "great to the ends of the earth" (Mic. 5:4). He would "bring forth justice to the nations" (Isa. 42:1).

Such a concept was totally alien to the Jews, and in some sense is still so today. They were to keep themselves separate from all foreign Gentiles. They saw their God as saving only them. While they knew there was only one God, and he must be the Lord of all creation, they had no vision for saving the world. This came with the Messiah.

For Reflection and Discussion

1. What previous thought have you given to prophecy? How do you deal with the relationship of time and eternity?

2. Whenever you heard the Christmas story previously, did it strike you that prophecy was being fulfilled in a spectacular way?

3. Why do you think Old Testament prophecies concerning the Messiah center primarily around his birth and death?

4. In the Old Testament whom was the Messiah spoken of as ministering to and for?

5. What is the significance of the Messiah's identification with the needs of the disenfranchised, and the pain of those who were in need of healing?

6. What do you perceive was the key ingredient of the Messiah's coming, as foretold by the Old Testament?

7

The Evidence of
the Resurrection

Ultimately the Christian faith stands or falls on the evidence of the resurrection. If Jesus Christ really walked from the grave alive, his teaching takes on a different authority, and the realities of life take on a new meaning. On the other hand, the Bible, speaking in a blunt and realistic manner, says if Jesus Christ has not risen from the dead, "we are of all men most to be pitied" (1 Cor. 15:19).

In the face of this blunt reality, we consider the evidence for the resurrection of Christ's body from the grave. To begin with, there is no doubt that the body disappeared from the tomb. Though a great stone was set in the opening, sealed, and a guard placed at the grave, the body disappeared (Matt. 27:57–66). Neither is there any doubt that the message of Jesus, alive again after death and burial, was at the heart of what the early Christians had to say. Nor yet is there any question about the success of their message.

> Within twenty years the claim of these Galilean peasants had disrupted the Jewish church and impressed itself upon every town in the Eastern Littoral of the Mediterranean from Caesarea to Troas. In less than fifty years it had begun to threaten the peace of the Roman empire.[1]

All this in the face of determined opposition. In A.D. 35 a great persecution broke out against the Christians. One by the name of Stephen was the first to die (Acts 7:54–8:3), and then followed a systematic hounding of Christians who scattered to the four winds, taking the resurrection message with them. At the center of this opposition was a devout and committed Jew and Pharisee known as Saul of Tarsus. He was the equivalent of a university graduate and, by his own later admission, ahead of any in his own time as a Pharisaic Jew (Gal. 1:14).

Evidence from the Opposition—Saul of Tarsus

It was just a little after the persecution broke out in A.D. 35 that Saul was on his way to Damascus from Jerusalem. He was pursuing the Christians who had fled there, but also wanted to stamp out quickly the growing Christian movement in that city. While traveling on the Damascus road something happened which redirected the whole of his energy from persecuting the Christians to promoting Christ. The evidence points clearly to his having met the risen and living Jesus himself. He became Paul, the "Apostle of the Heart Set Free" (F. F. Bruce) and primarily through his efforts the amazing news was published throughout the Mediterranean that Jesus, the Messiah, was alive. The direct implication was that God had certainly visited his planet earth.

Paul's witness to meeting Christ is the one I want us to examine in some detail. He refers to it on several occasions in his letters to the early church, but the earliest explicit and certain reference is in 1 Corinthians 15.

Galatians 1:12–17 is possibly an even earlier reference to Paul's encounter with Christ on the road to Damascus. It may have been written as early as A.D. 50, at the time of Paul's first visit to Corinth. However, it could be dated at about the same time of Paul's writing to Corinth from Ephesus. The Epistles to the Thessalonians are estimated to be Paul's earliest, A.D. 50–52, written from Corinth. They make reference to the resurrection (1 Thess. 4:14), but there is no explicit description of Paul meeting Christ. Of course, the letter is alive with Paul's relationship and surrender to the living Christ.

We know from our study of history that Paul first preached in Corinth in A.D. 50. He stayed there for eighteen months both teaching and working as a tentmaker to support himself. It was not until the spring of A.D. 52 that he left and, after a brief visit in Ephesus, made his way back to Antioch, his home base.[2] While in Ephesus he promised to return on another occasion and stay longer with them. He managed to get back to Ephesus that same year. "Paul came in the later summer of A.D. 52 and stayed there for the best part of three years, directing the evangelization of Ephesus itself and the province as a whole."[3] (See Acts 19.) It was during this time that he wrote a letter to the Corinthian church that we now know as 1 Corinthians. In 15:3–9 are these words: "For I delivered to you as of first importance what I also received, that Christ died for our sins in accordance with the scriptures, that he was buried, that he was raised on the third day in accordance with the scriptures, and that he appeared to Cephas, then to the twelve. Then he appeared to more than five hundred brethren at one time, most of whom are still alive, though some have fallen asleep. Then he appeared to James, then to all the apostles. Last of all, as to one untimely born, he appeared also to me. For I am the least of the apostles, unfit to be called an apostle, because I persecuted the church of God."

The complete record of his encounter with the risen Christ is found in Acts 9. The earliest dating of the actual writing of the Acts of the Apostles by Luke the physician is in the sixties A.D.

The reason we go to all this trouble to establish dates is so that you may see, first of all, the historical reliability of the evidence of the resurrection. You often hear the glib comment that the account of that resurrection was written so long after the actual event, like a hundred years or so afterwards, that it must be distorted by myth and discrepancy. Nothing could be more untrue. Let me list the dates set before you.

A.D. 35	Paul converted
A.D. 46	Paul called to be a missionary
A.D. 47–49	Spent mostly in Syria and Cilicia (see Gal. 1:21)
A.D. 50	Arrives in Corinth
A.D. 52–55	Writes to Corinth from Ephesus

In 1 Corinthians Paul is writing only eighteen to twenty years after he himself has seen Jesus. But you notice that what he writes he has already preached in Corinth some five years earlier. So it was thirteen to eighteen years prior to his preaching to the Corinthians that Paul saw Christ.

At this point, I want to stop and ask you, Can you remember where you were or what you were doing when you heard the news that John F. Kennedy had been assassinated? How long ago was that? It was November the 22nd, 1963, over twenty-five years ago. And I can remember exactly where I was at the moment of hearing that dreadful news.

In some audiences I have also asked the same question about the day Pearl Harbor was bombed, and even more hearers have indicated their clear remembrance of getting that news—which is now over fifty years ago! In a more joyful vein I have asked some audiences about remembering their wedding day and honeymoon!

As Paul preached in Corinth he was recalling a life-changing event that happened closer to the moment of his speaking than the death of John F. Kennedy is to the moment of your reading this—let alone Pearl Harbor, or, perhaps, your wedding day!

The other reason we look at Paul so carefully is that he was adamantly opposed to the Christians' claim that Jesus had been resurrected. He was not a peasant devotee pining for a lost hope, and psychologically disposed to believe any wispy straw of evidence. He had stood by at the first martyr's death (Acts 8:1). He also understood clearly the claim of those Christians. It meant for him, should they be right about Christ, that not only was the direction of his religious belief way off course but that he had actually shared in the execution of one who was innocent, and indeed was in close communion with the true and living God.

Against all the odds he dramatically came to that conclusion.

> Ramsay believes that Saul's whole mind and conduct were based on the certainty that the imposter was dead. If it were not so, the whole foundation crumbled beneath his feet. Then, in the mid-course of his mad career, he saw Jesus, so clearly, so unmistakably, that he could not disbelieve. He saw; he heard; he knew; and there was no alternative to surrender.[4]

Others suggest that psychologically Paul felt full of guilt at the death of Stephen, especially in view of the joy and peace in which Stephen died. There was no denying the life-quality of the Christians. He had a growing sense of the failure of Judaism. The Pharisees had watched the ministry of Jesus, and Paul would have gathered this firsthand from Pharisee eyewitnesses. He must have been aware of something extraordinary. Saul in his reflective moments could not brush aside the evidence. S. H. Mellone suggests that while the conversion was sudden, there was a long period of "incubation" as Paul weighed his own angry zeal against the eyewitness of the Christians.[5]

How can we account for this incident having the admittedly historical consequence that it did? Why should a man of this tough breed and of this admittedly sane and virile mental caliber be uprooted in an instant from his cherished beliefs and swept like chaff before the wind into the dogmatic camp of his most hated enemies?[6]

The only realistic answer is that Paul met Jesus of Nazareth powerfully alive and knew beyond any shadow of doubt that the Messiah had visited his people.

Perhaps the most striking parallel to the narrative of Paul's conversion is Sundar Singh's story of his own conversion after a period of bitter hostility to the Gospel. Praying in his own room in the early morning, he saw a great light. "Then as I prayed and looked into the light, I saw the form of the Lord Jesus Christ. It had such an appearance of Glory and Love. If it had been some Hindu incarnation I would have prostrated myself before it. But it was the Lord Jesus Christ whom I had been insulting a few days before. I felt that a vision like this could not come out of my own imagination. I heard a voice say in Hindustani, 'How long will you persecute me? I have come to save you; you were praying to know the right way. Why do you not take it?' The thought then came to me, 'Jesus Christ is not dead but living and it must be He Himself.' So I fell at His feet and got this wonderful peace which I couldn't get anywhere else." It is interesting to know that according to the best of his remembrance, "at that time he did not know the story of St. Paul's conversion."[7]

Further Evidence

As in the case of the apostle Paul, so with Sundar Singh, it was not just the vision but the remarkable lives which each of them subsequently lived that sets their experience of Christ as doubly unique. The same is true of the other early eyewitnesses of the resurrection. There is just no adequate explanation of what followed in their lives, except that they had really had an experience of the living Christ. Would the disciples who had fled in terror suddenly be willing to risk their lives for a lie that they were trying to perpetuate? If they had stolen the body and knew it all to be a hoax, would they have died rather than own up to it? That doesn't make sense. Nor does it make sense to say that the Pharisees stole the body. Even if they had been foolish enough, once they saw that they were assisting in the myth of the resurrection, they would only have had to return the body and it would all have been over.

It is equally facetious to say that Jesus hadn't died. It was medically impossible for Jesus to have survived the scourging, then the crucifixion, then the spearing, and then to spend three days bound in a stone cold tomb. And in any case, even if you supposed this explanation to have any validity, the appearance of Jesus gasping for help and dependent on whomever for survival as he recovered would never have inspired a following such as swept Jerusalem. It would have been whispered by someone, somewhere, what really had happened. But there is no hint of a manhunt for the body of Jesus—dead or alive. Further, and one of the most remarkable facts of history, is that in all early literature there is not a scrap of evidence indicating a memorial gathering around the grave of Jesus. I remember when James Dean, the Rebel Without a Cause movie star of the fifties, died in a motorcycle accident, flowers were placed at the roadside where he died and vigils were kept. An anniversary ceremony was held there for several years—may still be! There is not the faintest clue that anything like this occurred at the grave of Jesus. Why? Because his followers knew him to be alive.

Yet perhaps more extraordinary still is the growth of confidence in the resurrection around Jerusalem. You would have expected the fishermen to return to their native Galilean countryside where Jesus had been so well received and done so many miracles and given the majority of his time and teaching; and there, in wistful nostalgia, gather the country folk into some sort of band of remembrance. But no, the Christian faith grew in Jerusalem where Jesus had met so vicious and dedicated an opposition as would lead to his death. It was not until the reactionary persecution of A.D. 35 that the dispersed believers in Christ were literally driven by the opposition to evangelize elsewhere. Even then Jerusalem was still the headquarters for the early Christians, and the church held its first council there some fifteen years later—A.D. 50.

Evidence from Inside the Family

Perhaps the most significant turnaround of those who were close to Jesus was that of his brother James. James became a leader in the church at Jerusalem. Paul, in his early days as a Christian, visited with "James the Lord's brother" in Jerusalem (Gal. 1:19). It is James who appears to have chaired the first great council of Jerusalem in A.D. 50. He certainly summed up the discussion and pronounced the sense of the meeting in the form of a "judgment" to be disseminated throughout the churches (Acts 15:13–21). Twelve years later in A.D. 62 he was executed as a martyr. This is recorded by no less an authority than the Jewish historian, Josephus, A.D. 37–100.

> Festus was now dead, and Albinus was but upon the throne so he (Ananius the high priest) assembled the Sanhedrin of Judges and brought before them the brother of Jesus who was called Christ; whose name was James, and some others; and when he had formed an accusation against them as breakers of the law, he delivered them to be stoned.

Now the reason we point to James, the brother of our Lord, as being of such consequence is that our families can be our severest critics. Certainly our families know us "warts and all." The one place that deception is least possible is in one's own home. Not generally spoken of is this fact, that the family of Jesus probably agreed with the criticism of some who said he was deranged. "Then he (Jesus) went home; and the crowd came together again, so that they could not even eat. And when his family heard it, they went out to seize him, for they said, 'He is beside himself'" (Mark 3:19–21). The implication is that his family was attempting to rescue Jesus, not from the crowd, but from himself!

The question that is forced on us is simply this. Is it possible that someone who lived as close to Jesus as a brother, and who was initially skeptical to say the least, would end up leading the Christians in Jerusalem where, after living in peril and surviving earlier persecutions, he would surrender his life in death as a martyr—if it were all a lie?

As we view the evidence, and there is so much more that could be given, the only reasonable conclusion is that JESUS IS ALIVE.

We have considered together, in fleeting fashion, granted, the reasons that Christians believe there is a God who has made himself known to us. There are works of greater thoroughness in each of the areas at which we have looked. But in the words of author Josh McDowell this is "evidence which demands a verdict." It is futile to be "forever learning and never coming to the knowledge of the truth."

For Reflection and Discussion

1. Have you ever before realized that the resurrection is the most critical factor in the teachings of Christianity?
2. Can you remember what you were doing when you heard of the assassination of John F. Kennedy?

3. What other outstanding memories are as clear today as when they happened to you?

4. What is the common characteristic of all these events that makes such an indelible mark on your memory?

5. Does the significance of James, the brother of our Lord, becoming a convinced believer ring true in your own family experience?

6. No one was easily convinced of Jesus' resurrection even among his most devoted followers. Discuss the skeptical reactions of the disciples as found in:

   Matthew 28:16, 17
   Mark 16:9–13
   Luke 24:10, 11
   John 20:24–29

7. Do you think that, like Saul of Tarsus who became the apostle Paul, those who are the most adamant in their opposition to Jesus Christ, are more likely to become the most ardent and impressive proponents of the Christian gospel?

8

Christian Confidence

In the church there is a well-meaning diffidence that borders on agnosticism. It is almost as if we have made virtue out of uncertainty. You often hear people say, either directly or by inference, that it is arrogant to be certain of what you believe. Some say outright that you are guilty of the "sin of presumption" if you know you are going to heaven.

I want to share the "birthright" that belongs to every Christian. It is confidence; confidence that we are loved by God personally; confidence that Christ died for us personally; confidence that he indwells us personally; confidence that he will never let us go; confidence that he holds us in the hollow of his hand; confidence that we have a destiny in this life; confidence that our home is in heaven; confidence that we can share with others, with our friends, and family. In short, it is the very confidence that God intended for his people that transforms the meanest and most ordinary detail of daily life and makes it full of purpose and significance in the grand context of eternity.

New Testament Assurance

See how the New Testament makes this plain: Jesus said, "I am the good shepherd; I know my own and my own know me . . . My sheep hear my voice, and I know them, and they follow me; and I give them eternal life, and they shall never perish, and no one shall snatch them out of my hand" (John 10:14, 27–28).

The apostle Paul put it this way: "What then shall we say to this? If God is for us, who is against us? He who did not spare his own Son but gave him up for us all, will he not also give us all things with him? . . . Who shall separate us from the love of Christ? Shall tribulation, or distress, or persecution, or famine, or nakedness, or peril, or sword? . . . For I am sure that neither death, nor life, or angels, nor principalities, nor things present, nor things to come, or powers, nor height, nor depth, nor anything else in all creation, will be able to separate us from the love of God in Christ Jesus our Lord" (Rom. 8:31–32, 35, 38–39).

Here is how the apostle Peter put it: "Blessed be the God and Father of our Lord Jesus Christ! By his great mercy we have been born anew to a living hope through the resurrection of Jesus Christ from the dead, and to an inheritance which is imperishable, undefiled, and unfading, kept in heaven for you, who by God's power are guarded through faith for a salvation ready to be revealed in the last time" (1 Peter 1:3–5).

Listen to the apostle John make it plain: "And this is the testimony, that God gave us eternal life, and this life is in his Son. He who has the Son has life; he who has not the Son of God has not life. I write this to you who believe in the name of the Son of God, that you may know that you have eternal life" (1 John 5:11–13).

The reason I quote at length from the Lord himself, two of the eyewitnesses, and Paul is so that you may not be in the slightest doubt about the New Testament teaching. The quotation from Romans is read at every Christian burial in the world almost without exception. It is one of the appointed passages in the Episcopal Book of Common Prayer.

Current Uncertainty

What a stark contrast is exhibited between New Testament Christianity and the tepid insecurity which passes for Christian faith today. Suppose the early Christians had sounded like us! Suppose the apostles had spoken like many of our present day preachers! Suppose, and here I take the liberty of putting modern jargon in their mouths, they had said, "Far be it from me to lay my trip on you." "I'm not trying to be dogmatic and I know everyone has his own point of view." "I don't want to put anyone else down, even by implication." "I know you're entitled to do your thing just as I'm entitled to do mine." "But you never know, perhaps Jesus Christ really had something; perhaps he was even God in the flesh. And you never know, but maybe he rose from the dead. Now don't get me wrong, I'm not wanting to come off as a fundamentalist, and the last thing I want to do is lay on you a Christianity that is narrow and literal. But, well, it's up to you. So long as you keep coming to church and trying to be good you can't go wrong!"

Do you really think there would be any such thing as Christianity today? Who would have followed them? How could you commit to such effete nonsense? If they had spoken in such insipid noncommittal terms there would be no church today.

One of the reasons membership and attendance in the mainline churches are shrinking is the poverty of the pulpit. In Pittsburgh, for instance, the Long-Range Planning Commission of the diocese in 1977 reported that the viability of close to 40 percent of the parishes was "questionable" or "extremely doubtful." Pittsburgh, I hasten to mention, is one of the healthier dioceses in the U.S.A.

The Confidence of Our Forebears

This book was written in the Bodleian Library of Oxford University. Not a hundred yards from the doors of the library is the church of St. Mary the Virgin (Church of England), where Archbishop Cranmer and Bishops Ridley and Latimer were sentenced to death for their faith. Nicholas Ridley, bishop of London, and Hugh Latimer, bishop of Worcester, died side by side on October 16, 1555. As they were led to the stake, Latimer said,

Be of good comfort Master Ridley, and play the man. We shall this day light such a candle by God's grace in England, as (I trust) shall never be put out.[1]

Just five months later, on March 21, 1556, Archbishop Cranmer, "the architect" of the Book of Common Prayer, died in the same way on the same spot. Earlier in his dispute with Queen Mary and the Roman church he had signed a recantation, a denial of his biblical faith, "for fear of death" as he said. But he went back on that recantation and publicly denied it, and as a result was led to the stake. A cross set in the road at Broad Street, Oxford, marks the site. As the flames leapt up around him, he reached down with his right hand, saying that the hand that had denied Christ should burn first.

These stand in a long line of courageous Christians. It is said that there have been more Christian martyrs in this century than in all other centuries put together. Africa and China alone account for most of them. It only stands to reason that martyrs, ancient and modern, knew what they believed. We, if we say we are Christians, are their spiritual heirs. But for the courage of the apostles and martyrs we would not be believers today. As Justin Martyr said, "The blood of the martyrs is the seed of the church."

It may seem that I'm advocating martyrdom, but what I am pointing out is Christian confidence. These men and women were sure of what they believed. It was a certainty which sprang from what they believed. Note again the Romans passage just quoted. "I am certain nothing can separate us from the love of God in Christ" is their uniform witness. None could snatch them from the hand of Jesus; he had said so. If you have the Son "you have eternal life," said John. He wrote to those early Christians, "that you may know that you have eternal life." No wishy-washy I-hopeagainst-hope kind of attitude here. That confidence can be ours. Individuals are crying out for it in their hearts, and the church is desperate for it in the pulpit.

God Wants Us to Know

When you think about it and are not just swept along by the well-meaning diffidence of the day, one thing becomes crystal clear: God wants us to be sure! If God really loves us would he not want us to know it? Love does not flourish in a vacuum of isolation. Love desires personal fulfillment. I am not just speaking of sexual love. It is true of any love for a parent or child or friend. Fulfillment is seen in terms of personal relationship and a deep sense of personal sharing with another. This cannot take place if one party is uncertain of the other or doesn't even know the other.

It may sound as if I am suggesting a conditional love where God loves in order to be loved. That is not so. The very nature of love is to seek reciprocation. Put another way, if God were totally indifferent to our response, it would be a clear indication that he didn't really love us. Love cannot be indifferent to the response of the one loved.

It therefore follows that if God loves us he will make it known in personal terms, God being a person. We don't want to reduce his love to a kind of heavenly handout. Nor, worse still, do we want to attribute to God the kind of misdirected parental love of which we are all very much aware, namely just giving his children "things." As our children need us more than they need things, so we need God more than we need a handout. Of course love means taking care of ordinary practical needs, but God being personal and we being persons, his love would extend beyond the practical to the personal and intimate.

Uncertainty Is Destructive

Also, uncertainty is of necessity destructive of love. I have counseled with men, women, and young people who are uncertain of being loved. Uncertainty breeds insecurity and insecurity breeds distrust. You can't love a person you don't trust. That is the meaning of the Bible verse "Perfect love casts out fear" (1 John 4:18). See the whole context of this verse:

> So we know and believe the love God has for us. God is love, and he who abides in love abides in God, and God abides in him. In this is love perfected with us, that we may have confidence for the day of judgment, because as he is so are we in this world. There is no fear in love, but perfect love casts out fear. For fear has to do with punishment, and he who fears is not perfected in love. We love, because he first loved us. (1 John 4:16–19)

Note the word confidence in verse 17. What is the basis of such confidence? Knowledge of God's love, verse 16.

So you see, those who in the name of humility and modesty promote uncertainty are badly misrepresenting God, and do you no favor at all. They may as well suggest that your husband can't be trusted and, in the same breath, tell you to love him and serve him and maybe things will turn out all right. What would be wickedly painful is if the husband could have been trusted all along and someone destroyed the relationship by planting a seed of doubt. I have seen exactly that circumstance in a marriage. I have also witnessed it continually in matters of our spiritual life. Don't let anyone ever convince you that God's way is a precarious tightrope of insecurity. "If God is for us, who is against us?" (Rom. 8:31).

God Wants Us to Be Certain

Perhaps the coup de grace is the expense to which God has gone in reaching out to us. It makes absolutely no sense for God to have given "his only begotten Son" and not want us to know. The very point of the giving was that we might know. It wasn't a gesture or token to satisfy himself or the hosts of heavenly onlookers. Nor was it a public relations ploy, which is often the case with much public and Christian charity. God did not just want to appear good or to appear extravagant on our account. He really came to "seek and to save the lost" (Luke 19:10). Put in personal terms, if God loved me, and Jesus Christ died for me that I might be forgiven and be made new in Christ, would he not most certainly want me to be sure and experience all he desired for me?

The extraordinary byproducts of this "blessed assurance" are joy and freedom; joy wells up in grateful praise and freedom to love back in grateful response. Again, take the example of human love. When the wife knows she is loved she is able to freely love in return; and, oh, the joy of it! Gone is the crippling and inhibiting insecurity of, "Do you really love me?" A child that grows up in the sure knowledge of parental love is free to develop a wholesome and creative climate of security. So it is in the spiritual realm.

Confident Christians are transformed and transforming. Marriages are transformed, careers are transformed, churches are transformed, the future is transformed. Pessimism is not a Christian virtue. Optimism is. Christian assurance dispels the one and stimulates the other. Just this change alone would free many a soul from depression. Without Christ there is much about which to be depressed. As pointed out earlier, depression is a perfectly healthy response to a hopelessly depressing situation. But convinced Christians see things through the eyes of Christ. "Through him who loved us," says the Bible, "we are more than conquerors" (Rom. 8:37).

Just imagine our churches full of people meeting in the sure confidence of God's love, a love that has transformed their lives and made them agents of transformation in the lives of others. Imagine preaching that springs from an overwhelming assurance that the God of the Bible is the God of today, and that his promises of love and reconciliation have not changed one iota.

For Reflection and Discussion

1. Can you identify with "well-meaning diffidence"?
2. Do you agree that too many Christians are infected by it?
3. Could it be that they have missed the teaching of the Bible on certainty?
4. Does it make sense that if God loved us he would want us to be certain?
5. What is frightening to so many people about such certainty?
6. Discuss the relationship between certainty and courageous living.
7. What good things might happen in our society if people were more convinced about what they believe?

9

A Faith That Can Be Yours

We All Begin as Unbelievers

Virtually everyone who comes to a living faith in Jesus Christ passes through various stages of unbelief. The most common first reaction on meeting a verbal Christian—one who talks about his faith—is antagonism. Often it's a friend who has gone through the struggles already and unloads with great enthusiasm what God has done for him. You can hardly believe it! The friendship is jeopardized and you are not sure how to relate from there on. I have seen tremendous strain put on marriages even when a husband or wife begins to talk this way.

The second phase is a mixture of information gathering and Christianity posing a growing threat to cherished attitudes and life-style. Perhaps this book was put into your hands by a friend. Perhaps as part of your search you picked it up at a bookstore. But it represents to you this ambivalent phase of finding out more of what Christians believe. And yet all the while you are terribly threatened and put off.

The third phase is a growing desire to find for yourself what your Christian friends seem to have discovered. You are almost thoroughly convinced that what they say has intellectual integrity, but more than that, the quality of life these Christians and "their friends" exhibit has become extremely attractive to you. You have pretty much resolved your ambivalence and are positively searching for a way to make an entrance into this new world of faith and spiritual life.

The Basic Menu of Faith

For many people, having come to this point is rather like standing in front of a great smorgasbord of excellent food and wondering where to begin. Let me share with you the basic "menu" of the Christian faith and perhaps save you some of the frustration of walking up and down the cafeteria counter in confusion.

The first thing to do is to stop and pray. Earlier we prayed the "Agnostic's Prayer." Now it is time to pray another kind of prayer. Wherever you are, be quiet in your own heart and see yourself speaking to God.

Dear heavenly Father, I have come to believe that you are the Almighty God who is present here with me now. Even as I pray to you I sense the temptation to step back and return to my doubts and reservations. I ask you to help me give my attention to what you have convinced me is the only way to live a fulfilled and joyful life. Help me to turn my back on the negative attitudes which have dominated my thinking for far too long, and to turn to face you. Please grant me to know the life-giving truth of your Son, Jesus Christ. Amen.

You may need to dwell on this prayer for a while. Make it a real conversation with God, and see yourself in private audience with him, being as open and honest in your heart toward him as you know how.

As we proceed, one or another of the following areas of truth may be in more or less need of further explanation for you personally. We each come with a different awareness of need from different struggles in our search for peace with God. For this reason I will spell out clearly each "course of the menu" so that nothing essential will be missed. First of all let me set before you the outline.

The Character of God
    His Holiness
    His Love
The Plight of Humankind
    We Are Sinful
    We Are Alienated
God's Action to Reconcile Us to Himself
    The Death of Christ
The Action We Must Take to Experience God's Love
    Trust in Jesus Christ

The Character of God—Holiness

Reciprocal Communication

We begin by recognizing that there are two personages involved when God communicates to us: God himself who initiates the communication, and we ourselves who must respond. It is this very situation, God being who he is and we being who we are, that colors his communication to us. Put another way, God is multifaceted in his personhood, just as we are. He is not monochrome in his character and identity any more than we are. But because of who we are as needy human beings there are two aspects of God's revealed character which have an immediate impact on us: his awe-inspiring purity and his overwhelming love.

The Holiness of God

In the Bible, whenever people were confronted by the living God, the first thing which seized their hearts was his utter holiness. For instance, Moses, to whom God revealed himself in a desert wilderness "in a flame of fire" (Exod. 3:2),

heard these words, "Do not come near; put off your shoes
from your feet, for the place on which you are standing is
holy ground" (Exod. 3:5). And Moses' response was to hide
"his face, for he was afraid to look at God" (Exod. 3:6).
Read also Isaiah chapter 6:

> In the year that King Uzziah died I saw the Lord sitting upon
> a throne, high and lifted up; and his train filled the temple.
> Above him stood the seraphim; each had six wings: with two
> he covered his face, and with two he covered his feet, and
> with two he flew. And one called to another and said: "Holy,
> holy, holy is the LORD of hosts; the whole earth is full of his
> glory." And the foundations of the thresholds shook at the
> voice of him who called, and the house was filled with
> smoke. And I said: "Woe is me! For I am lost; for I am a man
> of unclean lips, and I dwell in the midst of a people of un-
> clean lips; for my eyes have seen the King, the LORD of hosts!"

Notice how in the presence of God the seraphim, which
literally means "burning ones," hide their faces and their
feet from the presence of the living God. Hear their reverberating calls of worship, "Holy, holy, holy is the LORD of
hosts; the whole earth is full of his glory." And hear Isaiah's
cry, "Woe is me! For I am lost."

When Saul of Tarsus met the risen Lord Jesus on the road
to Damascus, it was in the form of a "blinding light" (Acts
9:3–8). The Bible sums it up this way, "God is light and in
him is no darkness at all" (1 John 1:5).

The Meaning of Holiness

In simple straightforward terms, God's holiness means
three things:

First, it means God is morally perfect. He is in himself
the expression of all perfection. His commandments then
are not arbitrary, as if he could change them at whim, that
is, change the rules of the game because we messed it all
up and wouldn't play it right. He is not like the lawmakers

who, because the vast majority of people flout a given law, simply change it to accommodate their behavior and thereby protect the integrity of the law.

Nor does God grade on the curve; that is, take the median of human behavior and use it as the standard by which he will judge everyone. He does not have a book called Situation Ethics in his library.

Right is right and wrong is wrong, not primarily because God says so, but because of who he is and what he is like. It is because of what God is like that he says what he says. The world is not a vast Monopoly game he has designed, making up rules just so there can be winners and losers. His expressed standards for the way we should live, spring from his very nature—who he is.

Second, it means God is perfectly just. Not only is his standard perfection but he weighs and judges all things perfectly. His perceptions are not errant. He does not even make poor "judgment calls." There is no weakness that makes him respond out of defensiveness, or threat to his identity that causes him to act with rashness. He cannot be bribed. He is "no respecter of persons." There is not the slightest hint that, like our court system, there is one judgment for the rich and another for the poor. There are no legal technicalities which can ever divert the course of justice. All of us can count on absolute and impartial justice at his hand.

Third, it means that sin cannot coexist with God. God is utterly and altogether pure, and nothing corrupt, warped, or sinful can coexist in the rarefied climate of his presence. Just as certain living organisms cannot live in the light of the sun, no more can sinful men and women in the brightness of his holiness.

Experience of Holiness and Evil

Many can bear witness to the chilling fear of the presence of evil. The nightmare is a universal experience. But how many have been awestruck by holiness? Have you ever wondered about the fascination with horror movies? When did you last see a film that tried to capture the nature of holiness? There are many authors who can paralyze us with the fear and horror of evil. Which author can you name who has inspired you with his portrayal of holiness?

The truth is that we know plenty about evil because it is everywhere present. We know very little about holiness, until God in his mercy begins to show himself to us. Perhaps it is that we can handle the horror of evil better than the sheer intimidation of holiness.

And yet, sooner or later there is an aching in the human heart for the beauty of holiness, the desire "to be pure as he is pure." The original image in which we were created, namely that of the living God, still lingers as a distant memory and longing. We have inherited vestiges of what God meant us to be, and by them, deep reaches out to deep to bring us to himself.

The Character of God—Love

This is the second and overwhelming side of God's character. God said to his chosen people, Israel, "I have loved you with an everlasting love." The author who said, "God is light," also says, "God is love" (1 John 1:5; 4:8). Perhaps the most famous verse of the Bible is the one which begins, "God so loved the world . . ." (John 3:16).

It is the love of God that reaches out in mercy. "There is forgiveness with thee," says Psalm 130:4; and in Daniel 9 we read "to the Lord our God belong mercy and forgiveness" (v. 9). In the Bible the single most constant expression of God's love is his desire to forgive and the lengths to which he has gone in order that we might be forgiven. His "steadfast love" is nearly always expressed in terms of his offer of forgiveness.

The Dilemma of Love and Justice

These two characteristics, God's holiness and God's forgiveness, seem to be incompatible. On the one hand the holiness of God drives us away in judgment, but on the other hand his mercy bids us come and be forgiven. If God is to be just, how can he be merciful? If he is to be merciful, how can he be just? It appears that if he is to be just he must close off his mercy, and if he is to be merciful he must deny his justice. We will return to this dilemma in a moment, but first we must consider one other problem.

The Plight of Humankind—Sinful

Missing the Mark

In the light of whom God has revealed himself to be, we now review the character of humankind. The reason we are so threatened by the holiness of God is that we are sinful. After a muddy game of football, a player may not feel out of place alongside all the other muddy players, but take him to the head table of a formal banquet and he will feel conspicuous in the extreme. Similarly, one man judged alongside another may feel perfectly content, but in the presence of the God we have just described he only wants to get away as soon as possible. And when there is no place to which he can run, then all he can do is hide his face.

All Are Sinful

The Bible says we "all have sinned and fall short of the glory of God" (Rom. 3:23). Sin, then, is not just seen in the odious terms of murder, rape, or robbery, but in terms of falling short of God's glory. The English word sin has its origin in the ancient sport of archery. When an archer was shooting long distances at a target, a man would call and tell him if he had missed or not. When he missed, the call to the archer was "sin." You have missed the mark.

Further, the Bible tells us that we are "all sinners." We

have all missed the mark. "None is righteous, no, not one" (Rom. 3:10). That is, not one of us is perfect the way God is perfect.

The Gravity of Sin

It is not difficult to come to terms with our being sinners. What is difficult is coming to terms with sin's gravity. For the Bible makes it plain that "the wages of sin is death" (Rom. 6:23); not physical death, but spiritual death. To people who had come to new life in Christ, Paul wrote, "You he made alive, when you were dead through the trespasses and sins" (Eph. 2:1, italics added). We can understand a little better the problem of this "death" to God, when we think of how physical death affects us.

Physical death is an affront and indignation to our human sensibilities. We hate to be in the presence of death and are repulsed by it. I have seen men angry at the knowledge of their own imminent death—men who all their lives had everything under control and could buy whatever changes they wanted to effect. Death was an invasion of their self-determinism and their dignity.

This is but a small indication of the affront and indignation that spiritual death is to the living God. This is one of the reasons that the Jew, having touched a dead person or animal, was excluded from worship until he or she had gone through certain rites of cleansing. It was an outward and visible teaching of how abhorrent spiritual death was to God. The statement "Your iniquities have made a separation between you and your God" (Isa. 59:2) is more than a separation as by a wall or by distance; it is the separation of death.

The Plight of Humankind—Alienation

Estrangement

So it is that we are, by nature, alienated from God. Spiritually dead men and women, of necessity, live in a state of alienation from God. Again, hear how the Bible describes it: "They are darkened in their understanding, alienated from the life of God because of the ignorance that is in them, due to their hardness of heart" (Eph. 4:18). Writing to those who had once been in such a state, the apostle Paul said that they were at one time "estranged and hostile in mind" (Col. 1:21).

The Human Longing for Intimacy with God

Now it needs to be recognized immediately that God did not create men and women to live in this state of spiritual death and alienation. And just as there is a haunting longing for the purity of God, so we want to escape from the loneliness that comes with our estrangement from God. Like salmon returning to their place of birth to spawn, so we innately yearn for the life and fulfillment for which God created us.

We may try many substitutes on our way to discovering the life that God alone can give. We may look to love, marriage, and family for care and intimacy. We may pursue career advancement for wealth, power, and identity. We may throw ourselves into leisure and pleasure for happiness. We may invest in the worlds of learning and the arts for creative stimulation and expression. We may sacrifice our body's appetites in order to be healthy and live long. We may enter the rigors of religious discipline.

In "Eleanor Rigby" John Lennon poignantly wrote about lonely people, wondering where they all came from and where they belong. Nothing can ever take the place of God. As Pascal said, "There is a God-shaped vacuum in every life." Augustine said, "We are restless until we find our peace in God."

What God Has Done

We have seen in concise straightforward terms that the living God, among his many characteristics, has revealed himself to be extreme in his holiness, and yet extraordinary in his love. These particularly touch our human awareness because of our human plight—we are sinful and our sin means spiritual death and alienation, and we long inwardly for reconciliation. It is precisely at this point we must turn to the earlier dilemma we posed—God's seemingly irreconcilable justice and mercy. We, on the one hand, are helpless to really change our own condition, and it appears that God, on the other hand, must deny an essential part of his character whichever response he makes.

The Dilemma Resolved

The marvelous news of the Christian gospel is that God has solved this problem in the person of his Son Jesus Christ. For in Jesus Christ God has come among us and done for us what we could never do for ourselves. He has borne the judgment we deserved, and expressed the reconciling love of God which we need. Once again we turn to what the Bible teaches:

> [17]Therefore, if any one is in Christ, he is a new creation; the old has passed away, behold, the new has come. [18]All this is from God, who through Christ reconciled us to himself and gave us the ministry of reconciliation; [19]that is, God was in Christ reconciling the world to himself, not counting their trespasses against them, and entrusting to us the message of reconciliation. [20]So we are ambassadors for Christ, God making his appeal through us. We beseech you on behalf of Christ, be reconciled to God. [21]For our sake he made him to be sin who knew no sin, so that in him we might become the righteousness of God. (2 Cor. 5:17–21)

In terms of our discussion let me summarize the salient points of this teaching.

1. Christ has taken our place and borne the judgment we deserved (v. 21), so justice is done for the crime committed.
2. Our alienation is done away with by God's reconciling love in Jesus Christ (v. 19), so we are no longer enemies but intimates of God.
3. When we are joined to Christ we become as new creations, and are able therefore to stand as blameless before a holy God (v. 17).
4. The two sides of God's character which appeared to annul one another respectively, his justice and his love, are both perfectly expressed and fulfilled in the one act of Jesus Christ dying on the cross.

Let me illustrate by taking you to a situation of which I once heard. In a little Tibetan kingdom, the ruler had established by decree that anyone found guilty of robbery would receive thirty-nine lashes. One day his mother was brought before him, caught in the act of stealing. Everyone knew two things: one, if he sentenced her to the punishment it would kill her and, two, if he let her off, his whole system of justice would be jeopardized. The people present waited to see which path he would choose.

He passed sentence—thirty-nine lashes—then stepped from behind his bench of justice and took the punishment himself. In the same way, when God in Christ stepped down from the courts of heaven and died on the cross, God was being both just and merciful. Justice was done for the crimes committed; mercy was extended in that God bore the penalty himself, so that we might be forgiven.

What We Must Do

Exercise Faith

There is a necessary response on our part to the initiative God has taken. There is nothing automatic. God has purchased a valuable gift for us, but we must receive it. The means whereby we lay hands on forgiveness and the gift of eternal life is faith. "Believe in the Lord Jesus, and you will be saved" (Acts 16:31).

Since faith is a very difficult concept for many people to grasp, we will need to spend a little more time looking at it. It is important to know how to respond properly to God's amazing offer of love.

Faith Is Inherent in God's Character

To begin with, I have often asked myself why God has chosen to make faith the means of not only receiving his love and forgiveness, but also the means by which we continue to live in relationship to himself. I have drawn the conclusion that faith is not an arbitrary scheme invented by God but part of God's very existence, and it expresses the nature of his being.

It is not within the confines of this book to delve into the triune personhood of God—Father, Son, Holy Spirit. But suffice it to say that within the "one Godhead" are three persons, and before God ever created humankind, his own existence was lived out in mutual interpersonal fidelity or faith. The Bible teaches that even when we are "unfaithful," God remains faithful. "He cannot deny himself" (2 Tim. 2:13). The characteristic of God's nature is faithfulness. As God has revealed himself in the recorded history of the Bible, he did it as a God who makes trust agreements and "keeps covenant" (Deut. 7:9). That is, he remains steadfastly faithful to his pledge or promise.

Faith Is Inherent in Human Character

When God created human beings, he did so saying, "Let us make man in our image, after our likeness" (Gen. 1:26). The nature of our existence then, created as it is in the image of God, has the potential and impetus to exercise faith. Our fundamental relationships cannot exist without trust. Husbands and wives make a faith commitment to each other in the sacred pledge of marriage. Parents and children, friends and associates, thrive on trustworthiness. It is the common coinage of all human transaction. Fidelity always affirms personhood, and infidelity always diminishes it.

When looked at in a broader light, faith sets free tremendously creative energy. It is the psychological means whereby the human personality is inspired to bring into reality "things which are not." It is exciting to see men and women accomplish great things through the exercise of faith, not in God necessarily, but just as an expression of human creativity and entrepreneurial vision.

The athlete who has faith in his ability is the one who surpasses even his own imagination. When parents exhibit faith in their children they spark achievement beyond expectation. A manager's faith in those he leads can inspire them to produce outstanding results. It is faith which transforms problems into opportunities and dreams into realities. Faith lifts human existence above the mundane and perfunctory, bringing to it creative challenge and exuberance. Faith is indeed "the assurance of things hoped for, the conviction of things not seen," and "by it the men of old received divine approval" (Heb. 11:1–2).

Faith in Jesus Christ

Let us see how in specific terms the Bible speaks about believing in Jesus Christ. "He was in the world, and the world was made through him, yet the world knew him not. He came to his own home, and his own people received him not. But to all who received him, who believed in his name, he gave power to become children of God; who were born, not of blood nor of the will of the flesh nor of the will of man, but of God" (John 1:10–13). A similar and graphic image is projected in Revelation 3:20: "Behold, I stand at the door and knock; if any one hears my voice and opens the door, I will come in to him and eat with him, and he with me."

Believing Is Receiving

Faith is described in terms of "receiving Christ." Note that receiving and believing are used to describe a response to the Lord Jesus and that each word in turn qualifies the other. To believe is to receive and to receive is to believe. Unbelief, by the same token, is understood in terms of rejecting Jesus, or of not "receiving him."

It is very important to see that belief is not mere intellectual agreement about Jesus. It is receiving him, embracing him, surrendering to him, depending on him; it is welcoming him into your life to fill the household of your existence.

Believing Is Choosing

There are many who understand clearly the claims of Christ but they have never taken the step of yielding their lives to him. So while in one sense they may say they believe, they have never done anything about it. What they understand in their heads, they do not receive in their hearts. It has been said that the longest eighteen inches in the world is from the head to the heart. Faith, then, is something that has to do with the will. Faith is not just intellectually accepting that certain information is true, but it is choosing to put our trust and confidence in that truth.

We can see this more clearly if we look at the three parts which constitute human personality. There is the mind with which we think; there are the emotions with which we feel; and there is the will with which we choose.

I know people who have an immense amount of knowledge about Christ but have never chosen to yield their lives to him. I have friends in the ordained ministry who have shared with me that even after their theological education was completed and they were ordained as professional ministers, they did not have a personal relationship with God. For all their formal knowledge about God at the time of their ordination, and even for several years into their ministry, they had not come to that place in their personal experience of putting their faith in him. They knew about God, but they did not know him personally. By their own admission it was not until they had been ordained and practicing for a number of years that Christ became a personal reality as they put their faith in him.

Similarly, I know some who have had remarkable religious experiences, and have been deeply moved emotionally, but they have never chosen to put their whole dependence in Christ. A perfect example of this is Lord Kenneth Clark, about whom an article was written in *Christianity Today*.

> Lord Clark has just published the second volume of his autobiography entitled *The Other Half: A Self-Portrait*. Sir Kenneth Clark (as he then was) became a household name around the world in connection with the highly successful televised series, *Civilization*.
>
> There is an arresting passage in his autobiography in which he writes, "I had a religious experience. It took place in the Church of San Lorenzo, but did not seem to be connected with the harmonious beauty of the architecture. I can only say that for a few minutes my whole being was irradiated by a kind of heavenly joy, far more intense than anything I had known before. This state of mind lasted for several minutes, and, wonderful though it was, posed an awkward problem in terms of action. My life was far from blameless: I would have to reform. My family would think I was going mad, and perhaps after all, it was a delusion for I was in every way unworthy of receiving such a flood of grace. Gradually the effect wore off and I made no effort to retain it. I think I was right: I was too deeply embedded in the world to change course."[1]

Many people I know would have equated this religious experience with faith and conversion. Lord Clark saw the need for a decision, and chose not to believe—that is, chose not to yield his life to the God who had granted the experience.

Christian faith is choosing Christ. Christian faith is receiving Christ. This is why Christians are called by the name Christ-ian. The focus of their existence is Jesus Christ.

Believing Is Possessing

Faith then is the means by which God, being who he is, has made it possible for us to receive the gift of eternal life. "For this is the will of my Father, that every one who sees the Son and believes in him should have eternal life; and I will raise him up at the last day" (John 6:40). "Truly, truly, I say to you, he who believes has eternal life" (John 6:47).

So it follows that when we place our faith in Jesus Christ, we have the gift of eternal life. It becomes a present possession. It is not something we wait for and may or may not merit at the end of our lives. When we by faith receive Christ into our lives we receive with him the gift of eternal life. He is "the life" (John 14:6). He said he has come that we might have "life in all its fulness" (see John 10:10). "He who has the Son has life; and he who has not the Son of God has not life" (1 John 5:12).

A Gift That Is Not Merited

Two other things become very plain in the light of this teaching. The first is that forgiveness and eternal life cannot be earned or paid for by us. Granted, we do not deserve this extravagant gift of God. To feel unworthy is perfectly normal. Something would be wrong if we felt otherwise. But neither can we do anything to deserve it. A gift is a gift. It is not a reward or a wage. It is a gift which we have done absolutely nothing to merit.

Secondly, when we receive Christ into our lives it is to make him the Lord of our lives. When Christ, to use his analogy, knocks at the door of our lives and we ask him to come in, it is not to stand in the hallway or sit in the kitchen. He comes in to transform the whole household with his presence and leadership. Every room becomes his; the "house" becomes the temple of his Holy Spirit (1 Cor. 3:16).

Faith Means Changing Our Life-Styles

This then, by direct implication, means we must turn our backs on all that he rejects. The word the Bible uses is repent. We don't ask Christ to come and live in a heart that is still determined to oppose him and have its own way. We have got to agree with Christ's way.

Further, it means that we must turn from all our sins which put him on the cross. We cannot seek his forgiveness with the clear intention of carrying on as before. When we trust in Christ, it is with remorse for all that put him on the cross, and with the resolve to live as would be pleasing to him.

It would be very easy for you to misunderstand me at this point. I am not even hinting that you cannot ask Christ into your life until you have put the "house" straight. Christ is the one who cleans us up and makes us new. But we do have to be sorry for all we have done wrong and determine in our hearts that we want to live differently—to live his way.

Faith Brings the Power to Change

Nor am I suggesting that you have to be sure that you are able to live a perfect life and never let Christ down from the moment of your commitment to him. It is the spirit of Christ in you that is going to produce a Christlike life-style.

Abide in me, and I in you. As the branch cannot bear fruit by itself, unless it abides in the vine, neither can you, unless you abide in me. I am the vine, you are the branches.

He who abides in me, and I in him, he it is that bears much fruit, for apart from me you can do nothing. (John 15:4–5)

It is his power and not our determination which makes the difference. What I am saying is that we have to be willing to have him do so, and want it to be that way.

So it is through faith in Jesus Christ, who died for us on the cross, that God gives us forgiveness. It is through faith in the living Lord Jesus Christ that he enters into our broken human personhood and fills us with his life. It is through faith in Jesus Christ that God has chosen to make us "a new creation."

The Commitment of Faith

We come to the moment of choice. It is possible for you by prayer to choose Christ this very day, and in so doing to be made a brand new person. "The old has passed away, behold, the new has come" (2 Cor. 5:17).

Let me lead you in prayer. If possible, find a private place where you can kneel down. See yourself kneeling before Jesus Christ. As you drop your eyes to his feet you see the marks of his love. As you lift your eyes to look at his face, you see him looking down at you, loving you as much as the day he died for you on the cross. Then say this prayer aloud, speaking to him:

Dear Lord Jesus,
   Thank you for loving me. Thank you for dying for me. Thank you for paying the penalty for my sins. Thank you for offering me this chance to be forgiven and to be made brand new. I give myself to you.
   Forgive me all that is past. I am deeply sorry for all the wrong I have done. I want my life to be filled with your power so that I can begin again, made clean and new by you.
   Come into my life, Lord Jesus. Come in today, come in to stay. Fill me with your presence. Drive out all the dark-

ness of my old way of life. Confirm in me now the assurance that I am forgiven, that I am made new, that I belong
to you.

Thank you for this new beginning. Thank you that you
will never leave me nor forsake me. Thank you that wherever I go, and no matter what happens, I am yours and you
live in me. Thank you, Lord Jesus. Amen.

As before, you may want to dwell in the presence of the
Lord Jesus, reflecting on the significance of this moment.
Look again at John 6:47: "Truly, truly, I say to you, he who
believes has eternal life." Jesus, in those words, says to you
that if you have believed in him, you have eternal life. Similarly, "he who has the Son has life" (1 John 5:12, italics
added). Continue to thank the Lord Jesus that he has given
you eternal life; that your home is in heaven; that your life
belongs to him; and that he has a purpose for you.

In being "born again" you have been born into a new family, the family of all believers. You have a new family in
Christ. In that family there are all kinds of opportunities to
grow more like Jesus Christ and to serve him. Continue to
thank the Lord for the new life that is before you.

For Reflection and Discussion

1. Do you recognize the route from agnostic searching to the desire for a confident faith? Discuss your
   own pilgrimage.
2. Which movie have you seen that epitomized your
   awareness of holiness?
3. What has been your personal experience of holiness? Contrast it, if possible, with your own experience of evil.
4. Have you struggled with the antagonism between
   God's justice which seems all-consuming and his
   forgiveness which most of us long for?

5. Would you say most of us have learned to excuse our sinful nature? What is the most common excuse?
6. Have you ever felt a deep alienation from another person? If so, how does this compare to the alienation you may have experienced with God?
7. Have you ever met a person who longed to be intimate in his or her relationship with God?
8. In the light of God's love expressed in Jesus Christ, discuss the first line of the spiritual "Were you there when they crucified my Lord?"
9. Discuss faith as the common coinage of all.

Epilogue

We began this book at a vastly different point than we finished. If you made the prayer of commitment your own prayer, no matter where you were at the beginning of this book, you have now inherited the Christian birthright of "assurance."

In order that you may grow in confidence and mature in your faith, I want to make several brief suggestions.

1. Memorize 1 John 5:11–13: "And this is the testimony, that God gave us eternal life, and this life is in his Son. He who has the Son has life; he who has not the Son of God has not life. I write this to you who believe in the name of the Son of God, that you may know that you have eternal life."
2. Read the Bible daily; begin with John's Gospel and read right through the New Testament.
3. Pray daily; prayer is conversation with God. While you will carry on a conversation with him throughout the day, there is for every Christian the need for a time of quiet and being alone with Jesus Christ.
4. Tell your minister and some other Christian friend about your newfound faith. This is the beginning of a lifetime of sharing the Good News with others and this is a good way to begin.
5. Throw your lot in with a church that supports and encourages your faith in Jesus Christ. This will mean regular worship on Sundays and taking the

suitable opportunities your church offers you to join in the ongoing life of learning and activity.

6. Begin a lifetime habit of reading Christian literature. This will help you to grow in the knowledge of your faith. Christian biographies are a source of great inspiration.

Notes

Chapter 2 *Quest for Truth*

1. David Cook, Blind Alley Belief (Glasgow: Pickering & Inglis, 1979).
2. Source unknown.

Chapter 3 *The Psychology of Agnosticism*

1. John R.W. Stott, Christ the Controversialist (Downers Grove, Ill.: InterVarsity Press, 1970), p. 13.
2. Dorothy L. Sayers, Creed or Chaos? and Other Essays (London: Methune & Co., Ltd., 1947), p. 25.
3. Ibid., pp. 30–32.
4. John A. T. Robinson, Honest to God (Philadelphia: Westminster Press, 1963), p. 19.
5. Ibid., p. 27.
6. Harry Blamires, The Christian Mind (London: S.P.C.K., 1963), p. 18.

Chapter 4 *Our Fundamental Options*

1. C. S. Lewis, The Screwtape Letters (New York: Macmillan Publishing Company, Inc., 1977), p. 11.
2. _____. The Great Divorce (New York: Macmillan, 1946), pp. 5–6.
3. James A. Froude, Thomas Carlyle: A History of the First Forty Years of His Life, vol. 2 (London: Longman's, 1896), p. 216.
4. Francis Schaeffer, The God Who Is There (Downers Grove, Ill.: InterVarsity Press, 1968), p. 132.
5. C. S. Lewis, Mere Christianity (New York: Macmillan Pub. Co., Inc., 1943), p. 30.
6. Schaeffer, The God Who Is There, p. 87.

Chapter 5 *The Words and Life of Jesus*

1. C. S. Lewis, Mere Christianity (New York: Macmillan Pub. Co., Inc., 1943), p. 42.

Chapter 7   *The Evidence of the Resurrection*

1. Frank Morison, Who Moved the Stone (Grand Rapids: Zondervan Publishing House, 1980), p. 114.

2. F. F. Bruce, Apostle of the Heart Set Free (Grand Rapids: Wm. B. Eerdmans Publishing Co., 1978), p. 255.

3. Ibid., p. 288.

4. W. M. Ramsay, The Teaching of Paul in Terms of the Present Day as quoted by E. M. Blaiklock in The Acts of the Apostles (Grand Rapids: Wm. B. Eerdmans Publishing Company, 1959), p. 87.

5. S. H. Mellone, The Bearings of Psychology on Religion (Oxford: B. Blackwell, 1939), pp. 154–55.

6. Morison, Who Moved the Stone, p. 143.

7. B. H. Streeter and A. J. Appasamy, The Sadhu (London: 1921), pp. 6–8, as quoted by F. F. Bruce, The Book of Acts (Grand Rapids, Wm. B. Eerdmans Publishing Co., 1954), p. 197.

Chapter 8   *Christian Confidence*

1. The Oxford Dictionary of Quotations, 2d ed. (Oxford University Press, 1953).

Chapter 9   *A Faith That Can Be Yours*

1. Stuart Barton Babbage, "Lord Nelson's Encounter with 'The Motions of Grace'" (Christianity Today, June 8, 1979).